Shikoku

Japan

A manga-blog springtime adventure

Karen Jennings

All text and artwork in this book are the copyright of Karen Jennings, 2024. The font used in the artwork is CCmarionchurchill.

All rights reserved. No part of this book may be reproduced or transmitted in any form or by any means, electronic or mechanical, including photocopying, recording or by any information storage or retrieval system, without the express written permission of the publisher, except for the inclusion of brief quotations in a review.

This book contains the opinions of the author. They are not intended to provide a basis of action for any particular circumstance. The author expressly disclaims any liability, loss or risk, personal or otherwise, which occurs as a direct or indirect consequence of the application of the contents of this book.

Published by Art and Soul Interiors
ISBN 978-0-9920826-8-0 (Paperback Edition)
Edited by Alex Jennings

A natural (and frank) storyteller, Karen effortlessly weaves practical travel tips and experiences into her narrative, meaning you learn while being entertained. As soon as I read that Karen's husband "Takes train and bus timetables a lot more seriously than I do", and that she wilts when faced with historical dates and periods, I knew she was a kindred spirit.

Sure enough, like me, she'll often head out with only a loose plan and a vague idea of what she might encounter in the day ahead. It can be a risky strategy, but also often pays off with intimate connections with the locals, their customs and the country's boundless ability to reward those willing to get off the beaten path.

Rob Dyer

TheRealJapan.com

The Prologue	6
Why Shikoku?	10
88 Temple Pilgrimage Trail	13
A Short Chapter for a Long Journey	18
Kochi, Kochi	20
Busy Busy MyYu Bus Day	30
Mount Godaisan Observatory	32
Chikurinji	35
Makino Botanical gardens	42
Rainy Day Cuppa Tea	48
Yosakoi Center	48
Kochi Museum of Art	50
Mall and Mail!	52
Sakawa Sakura	55
Makino Park	58
More Makino!	60
Ekin, more Ekin, and Ryoma	63
Ekin Museum	64
ACTLand	67
Sunday Market, Music and A Castle	74
Makino and Music!	76
Kochi castle	78
Dancing and Dinner	81
Train and Temple Day	84
Tosa no Yoakeno Monogatari	86
Iwamotoji	88
Beach Day	91
Sekkeiji	91
Katsurahama Beach	94
Matsuyama, Ehime	96
Feeling a Little French	100
Museum of Art	102
Matsuyama Castle day	104
Hanami	107
Kururin Ferris Wheel	108
A Tale of Two Cities	110
Ozu Castle	112
Garyu Sanso and Bansenso	115

Uchiko	117
Imabari Birthday Castle!	**121**
Nankobo	121
A Mizujiro Castle	122
Moving On, but Not Far	**127**
Shiki Museum	128
Botchan Clock	129
Ishiteji and Onsen Day	**135**
Ishiteji	136
Isaniwa Shrine	140
Imperial Bath Time!	141
Dining on Delicacies	145
Marugame	**146**
Marugame Castle	146
Goshoji	148
Takamatsu, Kagawa	**151**
Tanuki Tales Temple, and an Old Village	**155**
Yashima	155
Shikoku Village	159
There's a Haiku for Everything!	162
Ritsurin Gardens	**163**
Rainy Day Wanderings	**168**
Takamatsu Art Museum	168
Sunport	169
Takamatsu Castle	170
Sayonara Shikoku	**172**
Narita	**174**
Naritasan Shinshoji	174
Narita Omotesando	178
Sometime Later, Back in Canada	**180**
Final Words	**182**
More Books!	184

The Prologue

Kore ga ma
Tsui no sumika ka
Yuki goshaku
Is this, then, where I live out my days? Five feet of snow
(Kobayashi Issa)

A prologue to a travelogue! Somehow it just feels right. And that probably tells you more about me than you would think. I'm a geek. A nerd. An artist, photographer, author. In what feels like a previous life I was a research scientist. And then, somehow, a kitchen designer. Life is strange sometimes. I live in a land which is covered with ice and snow for about seven months, then becomes too hot and humid for the rest of the year. I'm here by choice, having left my native country with its valleys of green and grey, and lots of rain. I love to travel, boldly going where people have been before, aided and abetted by my best friend (he also happens to be my husband). He takes train and bus timetables a lot more seriously than I do, and I'm pretty certain I'd be hopelessly lost without him.

Me, Myself, and I

I've been to many interesting places around the globe and seen some pretty amazing things, but this time I'm planning a fairly sedate trip to Shikoku, the smallest of Japan's main islands. It's off the coast of Honshu, not far from Hiroshima, and is aptly named 'four provinces' because, well, it has 4 provinces. Shikoku has temples, castles, cherry blossoms and beautiful scenery, making it seem like the perfect place to celebrate a milestone wedding anniversary and a semi-significant birthday. I had it all mapped out a few years ago, and then, just a couple of weeks away from jumping on a plane... covid lockdowns. Yup. You know the rest. But now, three years late, it's finally celebration time!

Life At Home

I'm writing this two days before I'm hopefully setting off to Japan. Yes, 'hopefully'. Nothing is 100% certain at this point. Since first booking the flights four months ago, Air Canada has majorly messed with my itinerary, and it's all gone a bit mad. I'm still getting texts about flight changes, but I'm not going to panic. Yet.

If All Goes According to Plan...

It's snowing here today, but it's Ottawa. It's March. It seems like it's always snowing. I sneak a peek at Ottawa airport departures today. So far four flights to Toronto have been cancelled, but 10 actually left around the time they were supposed to. That gives me hope for step 1 in tomorrow's mega-journey to Kochi City. My flight to Toronto tomorrow will be ok, I'm sure. Well, maybe about 60% sure. Possibly less.

I'm about as prepared for the trip as I can be at this point. I've got my passport and other official documents, travel insurance, and chargers for electronics. I've turned on my earthquake tracker app, registered with 'Canadians abroad' so Big Brother knows where to find me if there's trouble, filled in online pre-arrival forms for Japan, and crossed my fingers that Air Canada will get me to where I want to go.

Today I have to see my physiotherapist one last time before spending three weeks walking around on a foot damaged during a fitness workout. The irony isn't lost on me! The good (?) thing is that Alan has damaged his knee, so it's unlikely that he'll be walking any faster than me.

I think it's probably time to pack my bags. I'm only taking carry-on, figuring if I don't check any baggage I greatly increase the chances of arriving in Japan at the same time as my clothes. Besides, it's only three weeks, and there's laundry rooms at a couple of the hotels. If you like to travel with big suitcases: plan ahead! On many Shinkansen you'll have to reserve 'oversized luggage' seats. If you don't, you'll either be fined or not be allowed to get on the train at all.

How to Look a Bit Dishevelled Most of the Time

Why Shikoku?

Any internet search will tell you that Shikoku (the landmass, not the dog) is the smallest of Japan's 4 main islands, and it's about 225km long and up to 50km wide. I'm not sure how useful that information is, but for comparison it's about the same size as Fiji or Wales, about a third of the size of Nova Scotia, and around ¾ of the size of Massachusetts. It's quite mountainous, with roads and train tracks traversing tunnels hewn out of the rocky landscape.

Shikoku is near Hiroshima and Osaka, separated from Honshu, the biggest island of Japan, by the Inland Seto Sea and the Kii Strait, and from Kyushu by the Bungo Strait. Need a bit of a visual aid? There's one on the next page! There are numerous ways to get there. I'll be arriving by plane at Kochi airport, and departing from Takamatsu airport. There are also airports in Tokushima and Matsuyama. These all have flights to major Japanese airports, but only service a small number of international flights. If you're looking for an alternative to flying, there's a number of passenger and car ferries connecting Honshu to Shikoku, including Wakayama-Tokushima, Hiroshima-Matsuyama, Tokyo-Tokushima and Kobe-Niihama.

There are three roads connecting Shikoku to Honshu, which at the time of writing are all toll roads. The Shimanami Kaido, which goes over a series of bridges connecting Hiroshima and Ehime, is the only one open to cyclists. The Seto Ohashi Bridge links Okayama to Kagawa, and The Akashi Kaikyo Bridge connects Kobe to Awaji Island, from where you can drive over the Onaruto Bridge to Tokushima.

By rail, there's only one way in and out – over the Seto Ohashi Bridge connecting Okayama to the Kagawa Prefecture.

Shikoku is divided into four provinces, and I'll tell you a bit more about them later on in the book. On this trip I'll be staying in Kochi City in the province of Kochi, Matsuyama (in Ehime), Takamatsu (in Kagawa), but won't be heading into Tokushima. I'll be traveling using public transport, but I didn't buy a rail pass for this trip. I think for me it should work out cheaper to just buy tickets as needed.

If you're thinking of visiting and taking a lot of trains around the island, the All Shikoku Rail Pass might be worth investigating. Like the regular JR pass, it has to be bought before you arrive in Japan. It can be used on specified Shikoku railways, but also on some trams, buses and ferries.

Where on Earth...?

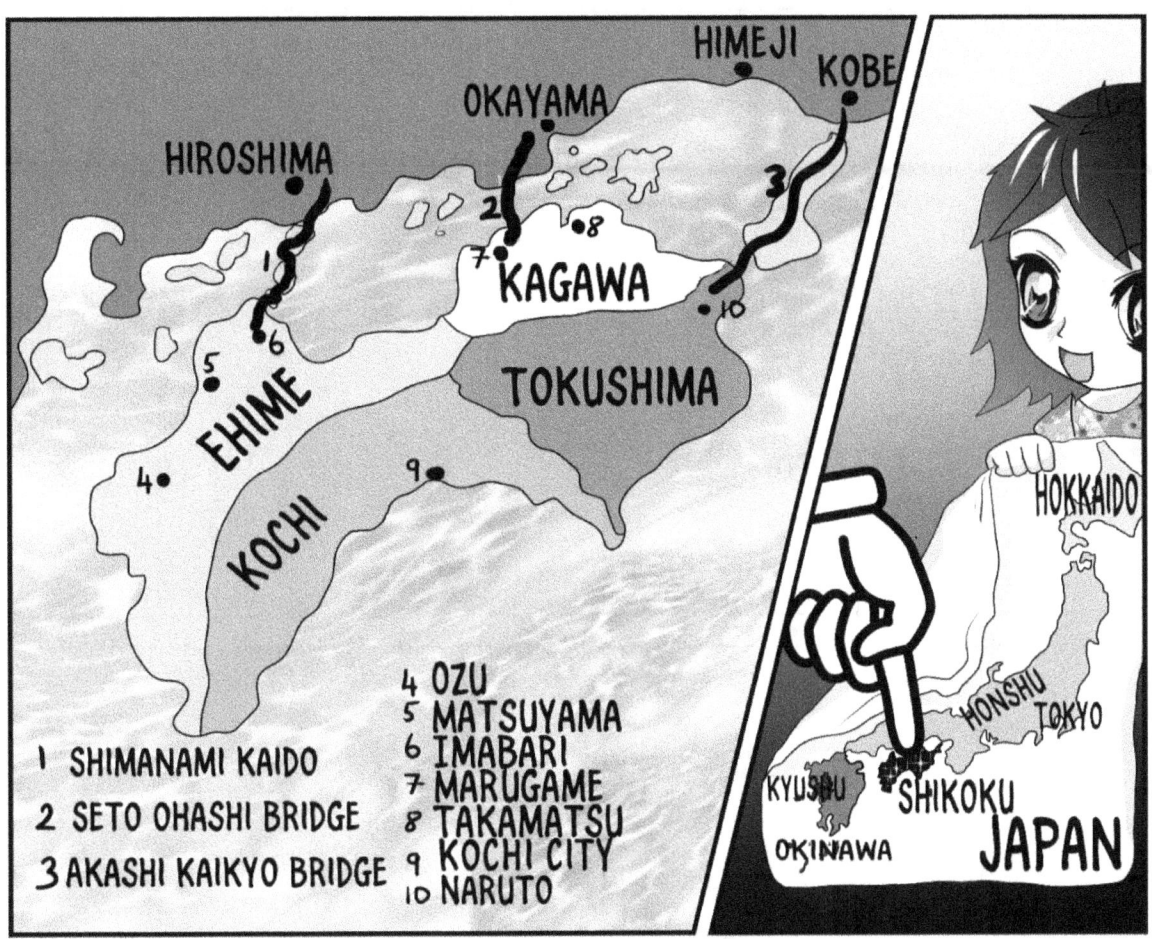

Shikoku is a popular place with Japanese tourists in the summer, well known for lovely hiking and cycling trails, clean rivers with rafting, kayaking and fishing, and hot sunny days. It can get quite humid, but that doesn't stop people from enjoying the summer festivals taking place across the island. Sounds like fun! However... I'm not going in the summer. I'm heading there hoping for warm spring weather, pretty cherry blossoms (sakura), and am expecting the occasional spring rain shower. Based on previous years it should be 16 to 21'C during the day, which will be very pleasant.

Oh. I've just looked at the long term forecast. It literally says 'tons of rain' for the day after I arrive in Kochi, with the possibility of flash flooding. It might be a good idea to find some waterproof shoes to add to my suitcase, especially if the predicted 46mm of rain falls. I know I've got some somewhere which I bought a few (maybe 10?) years ago when I first went to Japan. I don't have much need from them here in Canada. I'm usually wearing either thick snow boots or sandals.

Summertime Shikoku

88 Temple Pilgrimage Trail

Shikoku doesn't have big tourist attractions like the major cities of Kyoto, Tokyo, and Osaka, but it certainly offers an abundance of things to keep a visitor entertained. It's best known for an 88 temple pilgrimage trail (the Shikoku Henro), following in the footsteps of Kukai, who founded the Shingon School of Esoteric Buddhism (I have no idea what that is, to be honest). This Buddhist monk, given the name Saeki no Mao at birth, was renamed as Kobo Daishi after his death. He's credited as the founder of hundreds of temples throughout Japan, and was the author of a huge book called 'Treatise on the Ten Stages of the Mind'. There are many stories about his encounters with deities throughout his life. He died in 835 and is entombed on Mount Koya, supposedly not really dead but in a state of enlightenment.

The 1,400 km trail passes through all four of the Shikoku provinces, traditionally starting at temple #1 in Tokushima and ending at temple #88 in Kagawa, although there's no real rules about how many temples a pilgrim has to visit, or which order to visit them in. It takes devout pilgrims about six weeks (!!!) to walk around the island, sleeping outside in tents and henro huts, or maybe booking room at a temple or hostel. It's a lot faster, of course, to take a private taxi tour, or join one of the many coach tours driving Henro (pilgrims) around in relative comfort.

There isn't a strictly enforced dress code for pilgrims, but many opt to wear a traditional white tunic and straw hat and carry a natural wood walking stick. They're expected to recite mantras at the temples after washing their hands and mouth, and to light an incense stick at the main hall.

It's traditional throughout Shikoku for local residents to offer osettai (gifts of things like food, drinks, car rides) to Henro walking the trail, giving Shikoku a reputation of being a friendly place. You might also see gifts of food and drinks placed along the trail to help weary travellers make it to the next temple.

If you're interested in learning more about becoming a Henro, a good source of information is the official trail website at Henro.org. (https://www.henro.org/shikoku-pilgrimage). You can find maps, lists of places to stay, advice on etiquette, and lots of other useful tips and tricks.

I'm planning on seeing some of the 88 temples, but I'm definitely not on a pilgrimage. I will, however, buy a pilgrimage calligraphy book at the first temple I visit. Back in the Edo period pilgrims were required to get travel permits, and collecting stamps (nōkyōchō) at the temples proved where they had been. The handwritten characters are really quite beautiful, and I think it will be a great way to remember my time in Shikoku.

The Pilgrimage Trail I'm NOT Walking

A Little Bit of Useful Stuff

I've already used a few words in the book which needed further explanation, so here's a few others which may crop up. I'll keep it brief because I find things like this a bit boring...

- **Bodhisattva:** an enlightened deity who chooses not to enter paradise so they can help people on earth.
- **Edo Period**: 1603-1868. Also known as the Tokugawa period. Japan was ruled by Shoguns, under Tokugawa Jidai. There was economic growth, strict social order, and a long period of peace. Edo is now known as Tokyo.
- **Feudal Lords**: powerful local rulers and landowners, also known as Daimyo.
- **Henro**: pilgrim, often wearing a white tunic and a big hat.
- **Hirayamajiro**: hilltop castle surrounded by a flat plain, not to be confused with a Yamajiro (a hilltop castle without a flat plane), or a Harajiro (a castle on a flat plain but without a hill).
- **Jizo**: Bodhisattva who guard the souls of unborn babies and children who die before their parents. They're often seen wearing red bibs or hats to ward off evil. Jizo statues are also found along pathways, taking on the role of a deity called Dosojin and protecting travellers. Some Jizo statues are believed to grant wishes if they feel light when picked up while you recite a specific mantra three times...
- **_mon: for example** Karaimon / Otemon / Sakuramon. Gates of varying size and importance leading into the castle and temple grounds. Not to be confused with Pokémon, who also come in varying sizes and levels of importance.
- **_ji**: For example Goshoji. A Buddhist temple. Sometimes written as Gosho ji, Gosho-ji, or Goshoji Temple. Yes, I know that's Gosho-temple-temple, but...
- **Meiji Restoration**: 1868. Overthrow of the Shogunate and Japan's move to a more 'western' style of government under Emperor Meiji. Nearly 2,000 Samurai castles, seen as powerful reminders that the Shogun previously ruled the country, were either destroyed or abandoned in the following years. Some were rebuilt, some were destroyed again during World War II, some burnt down, some were rebuilt again...
- **Mizujiro / Ukishiro**: A type of castle built by the sea and surrounded by saltwater moats.
- **Tenshu**: The main castle tower, often described as a keep. Used as a lookout but may have also contained accommodations, reception rooms and storage areas.
- **Vassal**: Loyal subject of a local ruler, often rewarded by with gifts of land.
- **Yagura**: castle turrets or watchtowers, placed at the corner of castle walls.

Not My Favourite Kind of Date Night

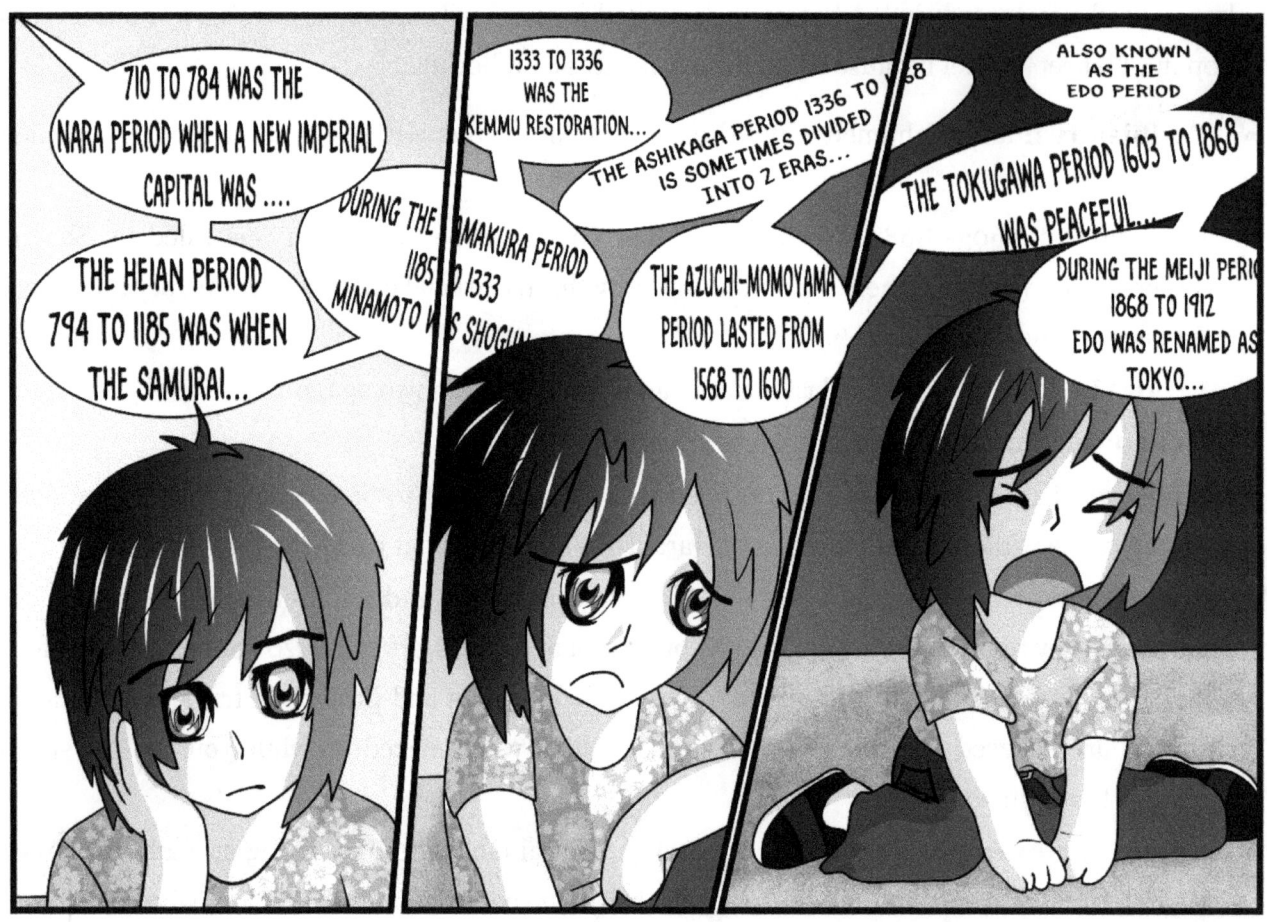

Language Lesson

I've been practicing Japanese in anticipation of this trip because English isn't commonly spoken in the more rural areas of Japan. That doesn't mean people don't know any English – I'm sure many of them do to some degree – but I've found it very useful to be able to speak and read some Japanese. Despite years of on-and-off study I'm nowhere near fluent, certainly not good enough to discuss politics or even read a newspaper, but I know enough to be able to order beer, find a toilet, apologise for random things, and get directions. Alan is my secret weapon when it comes to reading kanji – he knows about a thousand more than I do.

Throughout this book, please imagine that any conversation I have in Japan is totally in Japanese (very, very poor Japanese on my part) even though it's written in English. Unless you want me to write it in Japanese and you can use Google Translate if you're not fluent yourself? No? I didn't think so.

After Studying Japanese for Years...

A Short Chapter for a Long Journey

tabibito no
kokoro ni mo niyo
shii no hana
A traveller's heart is what you should emulate, pasania bloom
(Matsuo Basho)

I can't believe that after 3 years of waiting, the trip to Shikoku is actually going to happen. It's a bit less frantic than the original plan – I guess the lockdown years have made me appreciate the joys of taking life a bit more leisurely – and it's time to slow down and smell the sakura, literally and metaphorically. I'm aiming for a more relaxed pace than on previous trips, with more sitting in coffee shops, sleeping a bit longer, and generally chilling out. Alan is laughing – he knows me too well to believe any of those things are actually going to happen. But we'll see.

But first, I have to actually get there! It's going to be a 3 day journey from Ottawa to Kochi (thanks a bunch Air Canada), and I'm sure you don't want a blow-by-blow account, so here's a condensed version:

3 Days, 2 Nights, 3 Planes, 2 Hotels, 4 Coaches, 1 Taxi

Kochi, Kochi

hana-zakari
yama wa higoro no
asaborake
Blossoms at their peak, the mountain the same as always at daybreak
(Matsuo Basho)

Kochi, which used to be known as Tosa, is the largest prefecture in Shikoku, but it's the least populated thanks to the mountainous terrain. It's on the south-western part of the island, facing the Pacific Ocean. Kochi is hot and humid in the summer, has quite a lot of rain compared to other provinces on Shikoku, and can get cold enough in the winter for snow to cover the mountains. Most of the people live in small towns and villages arcing around the coast. The Shimanto river runs through part of the province, making it a popular vacation spot for water sports in the warmer months. The national parks are great for outdoor enthusiasts. I'm not planning on going on hikes, kayaking or mountain biking, so I'll probably not be straying far from the capital city of Kochi province, which is rather unimaginatively called Kochi City.

Kochi City is fairly small, but seems to be spread over a wide area, if that makes any sense? It's not like all the attractions are in one place, or easy to get to. A few are walking distance from the JR station, but most are a few kilometres away in once direction or another. It has the dubious honour of getting twice as much rain as Shikoku's other two major cities (Matsuyama and Takamatsu), and is the Japanese city most likely to get hit by a typhoon.

Getting around Kochi on public transport is fairly easy, thanks to the antique trams running north to south (the Sanbashi Line) and east to west (the Ino Line), intersecting in the middle of the city. There's a flat fare when travelling north-south, and an incremental fare when travelling east-west. For these trams, take a ticket when you get on (at the back), watch the fares on the screen at the front of the tram, and put your ticket and money in the box next to the driver as you get off. If you need change, there's a machine at the front of the tram. You'll see people using it while the tram is moving so they don't slow things down once the tram is at a station. If you need to change trams to get to where you're going, as you pay your fare ask for a transfer ticket. Do your best attempt at saying 'norikae-ken' and you should be just fine.

Kochi also has buses running around the city, the most useful one for tourists being the MyYu bus. It goes to major attractions outside of the city, as well as stopping near centrally located ones. All-day tickets can be bought at tourist information offices, and there's a discount if you show your passport.

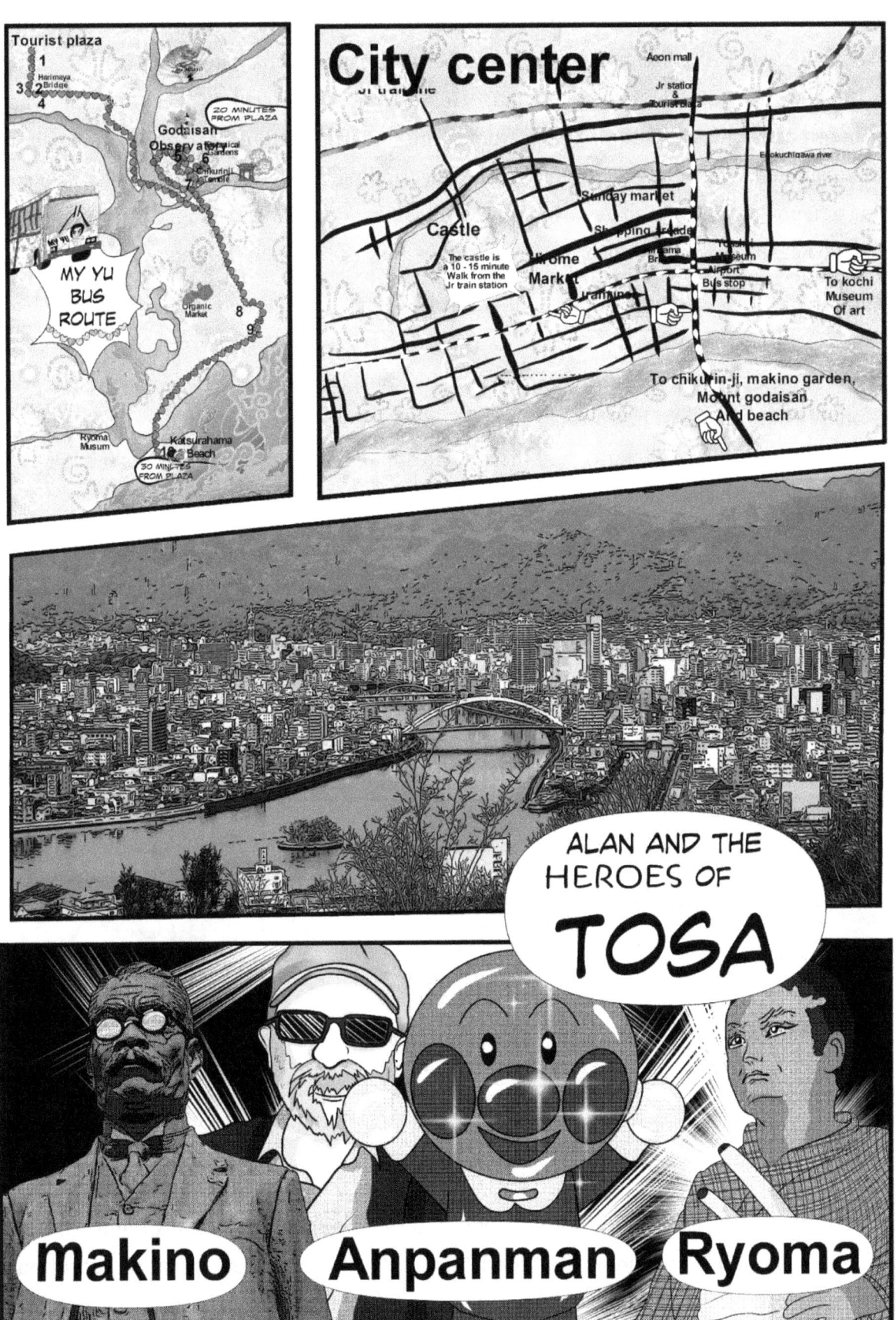

Jetlag in the Rain

We landed in Kochi around 1pm, and paused briefly to take a photo of Alan with a large Anpanman figure. You know who Anpanman is, right? A superhero cartoon character with a head made out of pancakes filled with sweet red bean paste (anko)? He was created in 1973 by Takashi Yanase, who wrote a series of books about his adventures which were turned into an extremely popular anime series called 'Soreike! Anpanman'. Our hero flies around in his cape, finding lost pets, fighting villains, and spends his days being a happy, friendly, good guy. He pulls off bits of his head to feed hungry people, and gets a new head when he needs one. But I'm sure you already know that.

We bought bus tickets from a machine outside the airport, caught the coach, and after a short walk in the rain we've arrived at our hotel. I booked the Dormy Inn because it's inexpensive, centrally located, and attached to a pedestrian shopping arcade. I've stayed in hotels from this chain before, and as expected the room is totally devoid of home comforts like paintings on the wall, soft fluffy pillows (you get one pillow per person, and they're flat and hard), and there's two small, hard, uncomfortable chairs. Did I mention that this place is cheap? The price more than makes up for what I perceive as shortcomings.

For most people, the best part of a Dormy Inn is the onsen (communal indoor and outdoor hot baths, with separate ones for men and women). Alan loves them. Sadly, drunks and tattoos are not allowed in the onsen, which rules me out. I'm very rarely drunk, but I most definitely have tattoos! In the past, inked skin was strongly associated with criminal gangs (yakuza), and while many non-yakuza people now have tattoos they're still generally frowned upon in Japan.

No Drunks!

So, while Alan can relax in a lovely, large, hot pool, with the spring air blowing over him refreshingly, I'll have to squish myself into our room's bathtub, which isn't deep enough to soak in, nor lengthy enough for me to unfold my (admittedly rather long) legs. I suspect I'll feel like a lump of blubber in a bucket. It looks neither comfortable nor relaxing, and from here onwards I shall refer to it as the 'blubbertub'. The really, really annoying bit is that I still have to pay 'bathing tax' at this hotel even though I'm not allowed to bathe in the onsen. Hmph.

After the mega-journey to get here I fear that what remains of the day might be a bit of a damp downer. It's pouring with rain (like *pouring*), so my small travel umbrella has been upgraded to a $7 full size see-through plastic one from the Family Mart attached to the hotel. Despite being totally knackered (a very useful British slang word!) I'm going to take it for a walk to Kochi Castle to see how it handles the weather.

It seems to take an eternity to get to the castle, even though in reality it's a short 15-minute walk along an uninspiring busy road. I'm sure there's more scenic routes, but in this heavy rain even they might look a bit dismal.

The large otemon gate provides a brief respite from the weather, and I can see the five-storey tenshu on the distant hilltop. Lanterns on poles define the edge of the path. There's writing on them – they're advertising a transport logistics company – but they're a bright splash of pretty pink in a rather grey world.

I look at the castle in the distance, and even though I know we'll be back here later in the week I decide to attempt the climb up the hill to get a closer look. There's a lot of steps. A LOT of steps. Alan is ahead of me, but he's going slower and slower at every turn. I finally catch up to him as we step onto the flat hilltop and stagger over to the edge to see the view. It was totally worth the exertion. The landscape is beautiful, with mountaintops peeking through the clouds, and shafts of sunlight illuminating the glistening rooftops of the city far below. A rainbow arcs gracefully through the sky, and a bluebird sits on my shoulder chirping merrily. Rabbits hop around my feet, and suddenly everyone around me bursts into song...

Nah, that's total fantasy. I can't actually see much at all because of the sheeting rain and dark heavy clouds. I'm tired, cold and hungry, and climbing the steps has been too much for my jetlagged body. Perhaps going back to the hotel for a nap would be a good idea at this point?

Kochi Castle Fail

But wait! This afternoon has taken a turn for the better! No, it's not stopped raining, and I haven't suddenly recovered from the jetlag, but on the way back to the hotel I spotted a sign outside a small cafe. It said *zenzai*, which is a traditional dish made from hot sweet red beans served with chewy mochi (pounded rice cake). It's the perfect pick-me-up for travel-weary jetlagged cold damp folks. I love it, so I decided to go into the cafe. The owner looked a bit puzzled when two bedraggled foreigners staggered in, and seemed worried as she handed me a menu totally in Japanese, but gave a relieved smile when I asked for zenzai and hot oolong tea for two.

Zenzai can be found all over Japan in the colder months of the year. You're unlikely to find it in summer, when chilled beans and shaved ice are popular treats to combat the heat and humidity. I first encountered it in Kyushu at a market stall run by ladies raising money for a winter festival, and I deeply regret that I didn't discover it sooner.

It's a popular dish! The owner walks by carrying another serving of zenzai, which she delivers to someone in the smoking room. A surly teenager is slumped at a corner table near me, playing on their phone and eating red bean soup. A couple of ladies have just arrived and asked for... Zenzai! It sounds like the name of a game show, don't you think?

Anyway, the carbs boost is just what I needed. I think instead of heading back to the gloomy hotel room I now have enough energy to wander around downtown Kochi until it's time for dinner.

Zenzai!

My feet have brought me to one of Kochi's main tourist attractions, Hirome market, which is easy to recognise by the large maneki neko (lucky cat) statue by the main entrance.

The market is thought to have been the idea of Hirome Shigeaki, a chief retainer who served numerous Tosa feudal lords during their reigns at Kochi castle during the Edo period. It was built in its current form in 1998 as part of a plan to revitalise the downtown shopping district.

This bustling indoor market is packed with fresh fish shops, a few meat shops, fridges of pickles, drink sellers and lots of fast food vendors. By 'fast food' I don't mean burgers and fries. The speciality of Kochi is katsuo no tataki – thickly sliced raw bonito (a mackerel-like fish) lightly seared around the edges on a grill over a straw fire.

The market is very... fragrant... in a smoky, fishy kind of way. The aroma hits me as soon as I enter through the plastic curtains covering the main entry. The market stalls surround an area filled with long wooden tables, and a vast multitude of people sit on the benches drinking beer and eating freshly cooked food. Most people have trays of katsuo no tataki, but there's also plates of sushi and freshly cooked noodles. A few people are eating odon – items like konnyaku (a squidgy yam product), fish cakes and tofu simmered in dashi – dipped in Japanese mustard. I can't believe how busy it is in the middle of the afternoon.

It's way too noisy and busy for me to cope with today, so I'll return at a later date to hunt for another regional speciality, wild mountain vegetable sushi, also known as Inaka (countryside) sushi. This vegan delight contains no fish, and is flavoured with yuzu vinegar instead of rice vinegar. There's even workshops where people can go to make Inaka sushi. I'm not interested in those, but I can't wait to try the sushi when I find some!

(Spoiler – I never do find any. Not in Hirome market, nor grocery stores, department stores, restaurants or Family Mart. I feel a bit cheated.)

Another regional speciality food is dorome, which I encountered the last time I was in Shikoku. The boiled tiny white sardines (about 1 cm long) with little black eyes were a big surprise (not in a good way) for someone who was just expecting a bowl of steamed rice in a dimly lit restaurant. In Kochi they're often served raw, maybe dipped in a sauce made from yuzu and vinegar, or with a pile of grated daikon (white radish). Believe me, I have no intention of snacking on them, even if they come served with a large beer. Alan is a fan of all things fishy, but even he's a bit hesitant when it comes to eating dorome. They're sardines, but to be honest they look more like tiny transparent worms.

The Flavours of Kochi

Well, it's the end of a very long journey and my first few hours in Kochi. I've had a brief soak in the blubbertub (as expected, the bathtub was a bit snug and not terribly comfortable), and I'm typing this while Alan relaxes in the onsen. I'm hoping he'll bring me a yuzu freezie pop from the onsen freezer upon his return, or maybe a chilled beer from a vending machine.

I'm not going to be writing much about our meals in Shikoku – I'm not anticipating many 'OMG I have to post this on social media right now' meals (not that I ever do that anyway), but tonight's dining experience was a bit of an unusual one. There's lots of places to eat in the shopping arcade attached to the hotel, so Alan and I decided to dine in a restaurant which had plastic replicas of food in the window, and a menu posted outside with pictures. As we walked in, all three servers stopped in their tracks and stared at us. Their reaction seemed a bit extreme, especially since my sometimes-frowned-upon tattoos were all completely hidden under my raincoat. One of them directed us to a table next to a fish tank, and put a menu in front of us. No pictures, and it only had one page. I glanced at the other customers and their colourful multi-page menus. There's something fishy going on here, I thought to myself. Or, as it turned out, not fishy at all. Whales are mammals, not fish, and our menu was the whale meat specials.

I don't know if the servers just assumed we wanted a 'gourmet' experience, or thought that we couldn't understand Japanese so giving us this menu would be amusing, or maybe tourists in the past always requested the whale specials, but I was way too tired to deal with this. I looked at the server. 'I'm sorry, I don't want this.' 'That's ok' he said as he gestured to the door. Point taken. We retrieved our umbrellas from the stand next to the door and left.

Our second attempt at dinner was much more successful, in a restaurant opposite the I-no-eat-whale-meat place. A warm friendly welcome, a menu with pictures, large cold beers, and a meal totally devoid of whale. Happy times indeed.

Having a Whale of a Time

Busy Busy MyYu Bus Day

omoshiro ya
kotoshi no haru mo
tabi no sora
Such pleasure this spring again a trip away from home
(Matsuo Basho)

I had a bit of a restless night last night, pinging awake at around 2:30am. I couldn't get back to sleep afterwards, so now that Alan has finally woken up (it's 6am) I'm more than ready to start my day. The restaurant opens at 6:30, so I won't have to wait much longer for breakfast.

The Dormy Inn breakfast, which I suspect will be pretty much the same every day (spoiler alert, it was) has a buffet of Japanese dishes and some western stuff like scrambled eggs, hotdog-like sausages, bread and jam. There's the local dishes of lightly seared bonito and dorome, and, of course, rice, miso soup, pickles, a variety of miniature pots containing tiny portions of vegetables, chilled tofu, and various deep fried things. I'm really happy to see some pickled plums (umeboshi). The ones in Japan are so much nicer than those I buy from the Chinese grocery store back home.

It looks like today is going to be warm and sunny, which is a relief after yesterday's downpour. The plan is to walk to the tourist information office at the railway station, buy some bus tickets, and head off on an adventure or two before it starts raining again.

I read somewhere that the information plaza is a tourist attraction in its own right, but I think that might be overstating things. Sure, the building is attractive, and there's lots of wood beams and flooring inside, but it's hardly a tourist attraction. It is, however, a very useful place, with maps and information sheets in a variety of languages. You can rent bikes here if you want to ride around the city, buy bus tickets, get information on hotels and hostels, and do all the other things you would expect to do in such a place. After the walk here it's nice to discover they have toilets for visitors. There's a little shop attached to the information center selling regional snacks and gifts in case you need to grab something at the last minute before boarding a train.

There's three huge statues of guys with swords outside in the plaza, one of which I assume is Ryoma Sakamoto but I'm not sure who the other two are. Ryoma was an important samurai from Kochi who helped overthrow the Tokugawa shogunate at the beginning of the Meiji restoration period. He was assassinated at the age of 33, but I'm sure I'll be seeing him again during my stay in Kochi.

Ryoma and Friends

I've purchased MyYu bus tickets, one of which is for the bus going to Mount Godaison today and the second is for a trip later in the week to Katsurahama beach. I got 50% off the ticket price by showing my passport, which was nice. I also got some useful maps in English and a couple of pamphlets for touristy things around the area.

Well, the bus has arrived and is now full of tourists squished into the tiny seats. People much smaller than me are shuffling in an attempt to get comfortable while pressing shoulders with the person next to them. Alan and I are packed in like a couple of sardines in a can and might need a shoehorn when it's time to stand up again. But at least we've got a seat, unlike anyone who will be boarding at the Hirayama Bridge stop in the middle of town. It's now definitely standing room only.

If We Fit, We Sit!

Mount Godaisan Observatory

After a rather cramped ride along city streets followed by steep, curving, narrow mountain roads we've arrived at the Mount Godaison Observatory at MyYu bus stop number 5. An observatory is usually defined as 'a room or building housing an astronomical telescope or other scientific equipment for the study of natural phenomena' or 'a position or building that gives an extensive view'. The Mount Godaisan Observatory falls firmly into the second category, distinctly lacking any astronomical equipment or scientific instruments. At the entrance there's a cold drinks vending machine and washrooms, and there seems to be a bit of construction work going on. Old reviews of the observatory mention a cafe, but it appears to have been demolished. Perhaps they're creating something bigger and better, but there's no 'coming soon' signs explaining what's being built.

Talking of signs, there's one you might find useful if you visit Japan. Toilet. It might be written in hiragana, (o-te-rai which literally translates as 'honourable hand washing') or in katakana (to-i-ru), but men and women signs are usually in kanji. You've undoubtably heard tales about incredible singing and dancing futuristic toilets in Japan, but I have some bad news for you. There's still plenty of old fashioned squat toilets around, especially in rural areas. Put your feet either side of the trench, face the raised section (if there is one), and make sure you don't pee on your shoes.

When You Need the Loo

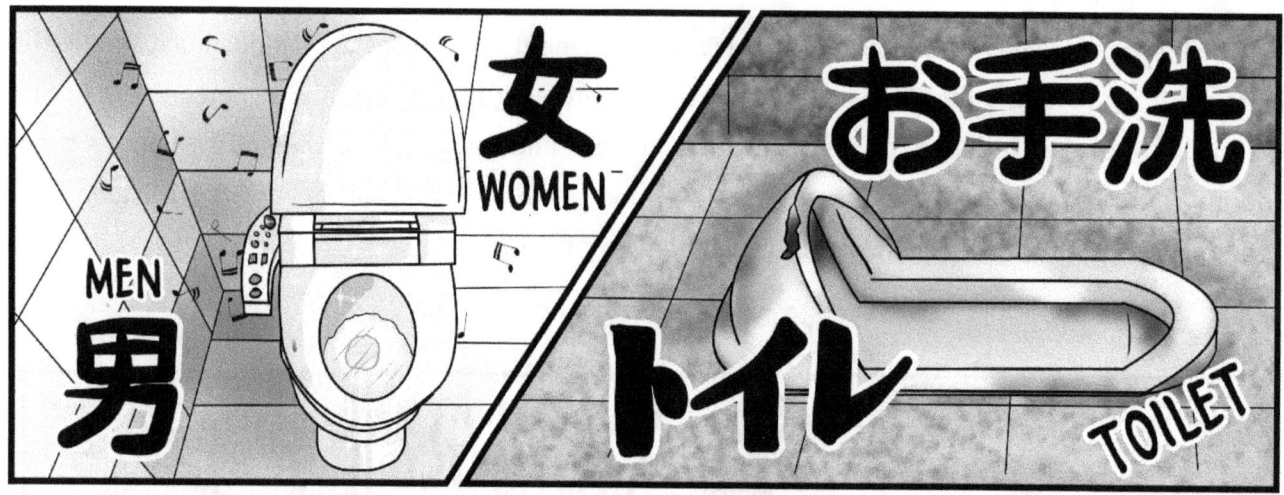

I head off into the gardens along a gentle path winding through a treed area with some impressively large rocks, pausing periodically to take photos of the cherry blossoms which are just starting to open. It's a bit early in the season (today is March 22nd) to see them at their best, but they're pretty. Apart from Alan, there's no one else here, so I can linger among the trees as long as I like without ending up in the background of someone else's photos.

The path leads to the edge of a cliff looking out over Kochi and the Kagami River. It's a beautifully clear day, and I can see the distant mountain ranges surrounding Kochi and seemingly random hills in the city centre. It's a great view, but there's nothing else to do here except take phots of it and say how nice it is. Perhaps one day there will be a café to sit in.

Back at the observatory entrance is a path heading off into the trees with a Henro sign pointing the way. I don't know if it's heading towards Chikurin-ji (my next destination), or how long the path is, so I'm jumping onto a MyYu bus which has conveniently appeared and I know will take me to the temple.

Observing the Observatory

Chikurinji

I get off the bus at the stop for the botanical gardens and walk a short distance downhill to the entrance to Temple #31 on the Shikoku 88 Temple Pilgrimage Trail. It was built in 724 and named 'bamboo forest temple' after a mountain in China, presumably because at the time there were lots of bamboo forests in the area. These days it's best known for all the maple trees which turn beautiful shades of red and orange in the fall. Perhaps there's a few sakura trees here too, but nobody seems to have written about them.

There's some historically significant things at this temple. The main hall is an 'important cultural property' and the reception hall is a 'prefectural cultural property'. The Edo period temple garden is a 'national place of scenic beauty', and the 'Meguri no Mori' area has a fishpond and a glass dome. The temple's main deity is Monju Bosatsu, (also known as Manjushri), a bodhisattva of wisdom, and students visit the temple to pray for academic success.

Entry to the temple and grounds is free, but there's also a Chinese style garden which can be entered for a fee.

Temporary Tranquility

Oh my goodness, this is beautiful! I've barely stepped inside the grounds and I'm already in love with the peace, tranquility and beauty of this place. Lush moss covers the ground, dotted with uneven stepping stones leading to various wooden shrines. Jizo statues wearing red bibs nestle at the edges of the moss lawns. Trees arc gracefully into the sky, and a few sakura blossoms on a small tree in the courtyard move gently in a breeze. A large bell hangs in a wooden bell tower, waiting for pilgrims to announce their arrival. I walk past the reception office and up some stone steps to the main gateway, guarded by two fierce-looking nio guardians. These legendary warriors are said to have travelled with Buddha and are found at most Buddhist temples, warding off evil spirits. Traditionally one has an open mouth and is saying 'a' while the other has a closed mouth and is saying 'hum', symbolizing the birth and death of everything. All I can say is that they're really cool! I've seen lots of these figures on my travels, and each one of them is unique. The nicest thing about these two is that they're not surrounded by the chicken wire cages I've encountered at temples in places like Kyoto and Tokyo, so I can actually see them properly.

Beyond the main gate is a courtyard, again with lots of moss, small shrines and trees, and a long stone stairway leading to the central area of the complex. I climb the steps, grateful that it's not a cold wet rainy day because I suspect the moss might get quite slippery, and arrive at a beautiful bright red pagoda.

A large group of pilgrims, who I suspect arrived in the tour bus parked at the botanical gardens, gather in front of the pagoda and begin chanting, some looking at books of mantras while others seem to know the words by heart. Not wanting to disturb them, I keep walking and check out the other temple buildings. It's all really lovely.

At the base of one side of the pagoda are innumerable Jizo statues arranged on moss-covered stone ledges, many wearing bibs or knitted hats. If you remember from a previous chapter, these protect the spirits of children who died before their parents passed away. People take care of the Jizo by dressing them in hats and bibs, often coloured red to chase away demons.

A large lucky cat statue stands in front of the Jizo, with one paw raised in blessing. It was placed there in memory of a cat which reputedly brought a local family luck and prosperity. My cats have brought me hairballs, shredded furniture, large vet bills and an occasional mouse if one tries to move in with us in the fall. Perhaps the next one will bring me luck.

As I stand admiring the statues, I can hear strange musical tones mixed with what sounds like bird calls, trickling water and other sounds from nature. It's enchanting. The source turns out to be a mosaic glass dome housing a meditating statue near a small lake, and it's a temporary sound installation by an artist called Insho Domoto. I wish you could hear it. It's mesmerizing. I'm surprised the pilgrims aren't coming over to check it out, but now that they've finished chanting they're heading back down the steps, assumedly to get their books stamped and head off to the next temple on their 'to do' list for the day. It seems like such a shame to come somewhere so lovely and not take more time to enjoy it.

Chikurinji Enchantments

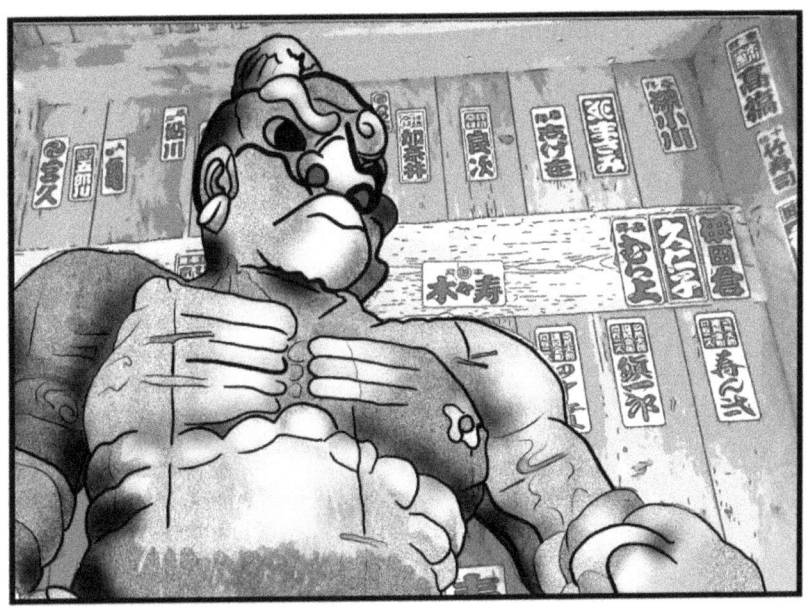

I continue my personal 'pilgrimage' around the temple and find Alan in front of a solitary statue in a small shrine hidden behind the base of the pagoda. It's a Hito Koto Jizo, which is said to grant one simple wish. Neither Alan nor I are Buddhists, nor believers in deities who grant wishes, but in this quiet, spiritual, secluded place we both silently make a wish for academic success for our eldest son in his current studies. He doesn't actually need the help of a deity – he's already got a degree and a post graduate diploma without divine involvement – but it kinda feels right somehow. Alan leaves a coin on the altar, alongside what I assume are osettai gifts of juice boxes and fruit, and in an uncharacteristically sentimental moment I place a Canada flag pin next to it. Just in case the Jizo would like to know where we're from, or something like that.

I wander back to the main courtyard and browse around the little shop selling charms and blessings. I see a shiny bell on orange twine with an orange blessing envelope attached, and I buy it to take home as a reminder of this lovely temple. Why orange? My kids are both redheads, so it makes me think of them.

Next stop is back at the main entrance, where I buy a beautifully patterned (orange, strangely enough) hardback book in which to get calligraphy stamps from the temples I'm planning to visit in Shikoku. I pass it to the lady in the office, along with 300 yen, and watch in awe as she draws intricate kanji on the page for Chikurin-ji. Three red stamps complete the certification saying I was here, and I bow as she hands it back to me along with an osettai slip and a blessing. My first 88-temple-pilgrimage visit is almost done!

As I entered the temple complex earlier I noticed a small building on the right with a sign outside saying something about hidden Buddhas and a secret garden, so I want to check it out before I leave. I pay a small fee to enter the house to see the Chinese garden, along with a display of paintings by Insho Domoto (the artist responsible for the sound instillation by the lake). It also allows entry to see 'secret' statues housed in a small building down the pathway. It's a shame I won't be allowed to take photographs, but sometimes 'you just have to remember' as I was solemnly informed a few years ago by a guide on Mount Koya.

One Wish Jizo, Secrets, and a Lucky Cat

What I'll remember about these bonus temple features is this: the garden was small, had a pond, and was pretty, despite looking barren this early in the spring. The paintings were big and had splashes of ink, and there was music, and they represented… er… weather? A stormy sea? I've forgotten already the details lol. But it was worth seeing. As for the statues hidden in the small building, I think one of them had lots of arms, and some of them were very old?

I think it's time to move on. It's been a lovely morning, but I had an early start and I'm hungry. I need to find lunch. There's what appears to be a mom-and-pop noodle restaurant at the bottom of the hill, so that's where my feet are taking me. It's hard to go wrong with a bowl of noodles.

It's All Downhill from Here

Lunch is great. I'm slurping fox noodles (aka kitsune udon: noodles topped with fried tofu) in the rustic, slightly ramshackle restaurant. I think the owners are more familiar with groups of pilgrims than random strange Canadians, but their dog thinks I'm very interesting.

Fox Noodles!

Makino Botanical gardens

I'm spending this afternoon out in the sunshine at the Makino Botanical Gardens, named after one of Kochi's most famous people, Dr. Tomitaro Makino. He's sometimes referred to as 'the father of Japanese botany', if that gives you some insight into what a big deal this guy was. I suspect this isn't the only time we'll be seeing his name on our travels around Kochi. So, what did he do? Well, in 1940 he published a book called 'Makino's Illustrated Flora of Japan', which is reputedly 'an essential reference work for both professional botanists and enthusiasts today'. It doesn't seem to be available on amazon.ca, but that's probably because it's in Japanese. He also collected around 400,000 botanical specimens (from around Japan, I assume, since he's the father of Japanese botany?) and gave names to over 1,500 species and subspecies. It sounds like he was one busy guy. Anyway, this botanical garden named in his honour claims to have over 3,000 plant species, including wild native ones and rare exotic flowers discovered by Dr. Makino. It covers 6 hectares (about 14 football fields?) and has various zones including a wild plant ecology garden. I'm going to refer to my own garden as a 'native ecology zone' from now on, and simply stop pulling up weeds. There's also a tropical greenhouse, and a hill with wild azaleas. Hang on a minute while I google that. Ah. Azaleas are a flowering shrub, and members of the rhododendron family. Judging from the photos, I have two of them in my garden back home. Good to know!

First stop, the greenhouse. It's big, humid, there's lots of plants including orchids and water lilies. It's quite impressive, but to be honest I've seen very similar greenhouses all over the world. I'm finding it hard to get excited about anything in here, in a kind of 'been there, done that' way. I want to get out of here and return to Japan!

Blooming Lovely

I think Makino's Garden probably looks much nicer later on in the season. Despite the sunshine, there's not a lot of bright colours to be seen today. The magnolia trees have just about finished flowering, and the cherry blossoms aren't fully open yet, and everything has that 'not quite ready to bloom' look about it. If you're planning a trip to Kochi to see flowers, perhaps leave it until mid-April at the earliest.

There's a life-size bronze statue of the man himself on a pedestal looking over the pond in the south garden, and I give him a little wave as I walk on by. He's sticking one finger in the air, but I don't know why.

What can I say about the north garden to inspire you to go? Well, it has nice views of Kochi.... and some handy signs directing wandering pilgrims to Chikurin temple. And I'm sure it's going to be beautiful in a few weeks from now.

I'm tired. Too tired to want to wander around the gardens any more (I've been here a couple of hours), so it's time to find the cafe near the north entrance. I need a sit down and a nice hot cup of tea. I don't think I could ever be a Henro walking to 88 temples. One temple, one garden, and I'm done for the day lol.

Dr. Makino, I Presume

Well, after a ludicrously expensive glass of iced black tea I'm ready to do a bit more exploring! On the way to the cafe I passed a pathway leading off to the left, up a hill. Turns out it's a flower garden. At, last, some colour! This is where I can demonstrate my phenomenal grasp of botany: there's some tiny violet flowers with white centres, a mass of brightly coloured taller flowers in vibrant pink, yellow and orange, some tall dark purple flowers, something wispy and pale yellow, and (drum roll) foxgloves! Nailed it! I'm sure Dr. Makino himself couldn't have done better. It was very pretty. But I'm exhausted (and still quite jet lagged) and would like to head back into the city now.

Instead of taking the MyYu bus all the way back to the tourist information office, I get off at the Hirayama bridge stop instead. This bridge is the stuff romance movies and true-love novels are based on, and indeed it's the basis of a folk song called Yosakoi Bushi. It's quite a catchy little number (my fave version is on YouTube, sung by Kanazawa Akiko) but it does go on a bit longer than I would like. So what's all the hype about? Well, according to legend, a Buddhist monk (for whom it was forbidden to have amorous relationships or get married) was spotted near Hirayama bridge buying a flowery hair pin for a young lady called Ouma. If you're hoping the story ends with them running away together and living happily ever after, prepare to be disappointed. Junshin-the-Monk was exiled, and Ouma was sent far away (wait a minute... isn't that kinda the same thing?) and apparently they never saw each other again. End of story. Closing credits roll while the folk song plays.

To be honest, I was expecting the bridge to be bigger, older, more dramatic? But in reality it's a pleasant gently arched wooden bridge with bright red railings, spanning a man-made stream about 25ft wide running through a pedestrian strolling area. But, luckily enough, there's still a shop nearby (with a large Hello Kitty statue outside) where you can buy actual hairpins, candy shaped like hairpins, and all sorts of tourist tack. We went in, but Alan didn't buy me anything. Nor I him. I guess neither of us wants to risk being sent into exile this early in our trip.

Love in the Afternoon

By now it's starting to get dark, and I'm getting hungry. Yes, again. It's not far to a covered shopping arcade, so I head off in search of sustenance. I think it's only fair to mention by this point that I'm getting a bit tetchy, and Alan isn't doing much better. We both cheer up considerably when I spot a large department store, the kind which usually has a depachika (a basement area with food counters and maybe even some fast food restaurants), and we head down the escalator. Nestled among the counters selling expensive cakes, chocolates, $40 bento boxes with local eel, and freshly baked bread is a stall making dorayaki. Woohoo! I love hot red bean paste sandwiched between two palm-sized pancakes, especially when freshly cooked. There's a couple of seats behind the dorayaki stand, so I sit down and enjoy the moment with a sweet treat and my equally sweet husband.

Just a little note while I'm resting here. It's not really acceptable to walk and eat at the same time in Japan. Street food vendors usually have somewhere nearby for you to sit while you eat your purchases, with garbage cans for any wrappers. Even konbini (convenience stores like Family Mart, Lawsons and 7-Eleven) usually have a small counter either inside or outside for you to eat what you buy if you don't want to take it home with you.

Ok, tetchy-snack-time is over, and now it's time to find some real food. I carefully study the list of floors on a sign by the elevator and feel quite pleased with myself when I decipher フードコート: *food court*! The top floors of mega department stores often have restaurants, so this is looking promising! Sometimes in the past I've been disappointed to find things like high-end children's clothing and large polystyrene boxes of very, very fresh fish (yes, right next to each other!) instead of a restaurant or two, but today I'm feeling lucky.

Oh Japan, you're so full of surprises. Today's 'food court' turns out to be a temporary store selling Rilakkuma merchandise. I've seen all the episodes of 'Rilakkuma and Kaoru' on Netflix at least twice (it's really sweet) so I'm quite familiar with the slow, cuddly, human-size stuffed bear and his friends. It's not quite the food I was hoping for, but I buy a cute Rilakkuma noren (divided curtain for hanging in doorways) using money my mother-in-law sent me for my birthday. I left room in my carry-on suitcase precisely for situations like this!

Bear Behind

I think dinner tonight is probably going to be a Family Mart special, eaten in the hotel room. Alan and I are both too tired to cope with a restaurant right now. Tonight would have been the perfect occasion to go back to our own little Airbnb apartment, eat onigiri and drink sake on a comfortable sofa in front of the tv, but I couldn't find one in Kochi anywhere near the city center. A room at the Dormy Inn will have to suffice.

Rainy Day Cuppa Tea

Hatsu shigre
saru mo komino
hoshige nari
In this bleak rain, even the monkeys seem to want little straw cloaks
(Matsuo Basho)

The rain has returned with a vengeance today after taking yesterday off, and the weather forecast promises heavy downfalls until bedtime, with bonus thunderstorms starting around noon. It looks like today might be the perfect day for some indoor activities! The Kochi Yosakoi Information Exchange Center is a 10-minute walk away, mostly through covered shopping arcades, after which the Kochi Museum of Art can be reached by tram and a short walk in the rain. Sounds like a plan!

Yosakoi Center

There's an annual Yosakoi (folk dance) festival in Kochi during August, which attracts dance teams from all over Japan and beyond with up to 20,000 dancers participating in the four-day event. The only rules the dance teams have to follow (they do their own choreography) is that a yosakoi-bushi song must be used as a base, and the dancers have to move forwards while holding naruko (wooden clappers). Apparently the performances are very lively and energetic, with brightly coloured costumes. A sign at the Kochi Yosakoi Information Center says 'you can experience the lively spirit of Yosakoi dancing all year round, try on traditional costumes, and make your own hand-decorated clappers.' Woohoo! Sounds like a fun time.

Well... It probably took longer to walk to the Exchange Centre than I've actually spent inside, but that's not a complaint. It's nice, just smaller and less exciting than anticipated. The outside is cool, designed to look like one of the trucks that can be seen at the festival. I've watched some dance performances on a big screen, taken photos of mannequins wearing costumes, and I've got a bonus photo of Alan holding some naruko clappers. I wouldn't go out of my way to come here, but since it's on the way to the tram stop it worked out ok. I'm heading down to the entrance to pick up my umbrella before heading out into Kochi's springtime weather.

Nice Naruko!

Kochi Museum of Art

The next stop on today's rainy day agenda is the Kochi Museum of Art, which I'm hoping will fill a couple of hours at least. It opened in 1993, and the photos make the building itself look really cool. It's based on a traditional wooden design with a courtyard, and it has a water feature in front of the main entrance. It gets rave reviews like 'The architecture is striking, using water to dramatic effect outside.' 'Inside is designed around a central courtyard with a shallow pool and a stage, where we were lucky enough to see an interpretive dance.' 'This is a very well curated gallery, housed in a striking new neo-classical building.' 'The regular collection includes some excellent Chagall oil paintings.' The museum website says 'The collection includes a total of more than 41,000 works by approximately 440 artists from Japan and abroad.' Sounds good, right?

Tramming

After a bit of a damp walk to the tram stop and a 15-minute tram ride followed by another five minutes of wet-walking I'm standing in the lobby of the museum of art. I narrowly avoided stepping into the 'water feature' on the way in, landing on the wooden walkway more by accident than design because there's quite a lot of rainwater sloshing around out there. And now that I'm here I find myself in a bit of a dilemma. After folding our umbrellas and putting them in the rack by the door, Alan approached the ladies at the reception desk and asked for two tickets. You know, like you do at museums and art galleries. The ladies looked at each other, then one slowly reached under the desk and withdrew a laminated card which said 'closed 21-23'. Today is the 23rd. Oh no! I looked at her in astonishment, and she kinda gave a little shrug. Apparently I wasn't the only person who didn't get the memo, as another lady approached the counter and was shown the same card. However, instead of standing here like a lost child she's heading off down the hallway, obviously on a mission of some kind. 'Do you think the cafe is open, even though the museum's closed?' I ask Alan, wondering if that's where she's going. So we're going to follow her and find out!

Hurray! The cafe IS open, and yes, it's where the other lady was heading, so the journey all the way to this museum hasn't been totally wasted. I'm sitting here with some soft pink bread baked in the shape of a cherry blossom and an iced tea, and Alan has been served hot tea in a china teapot along with an egg timer to make sure it's brewed to perfection. We'll be sitting here until we work out what to do with the rest of our day, watching the rain through the large windows.

A Nice Hot Cup of Tea on a Rainy Day

I have to admit that, in retrospect, a hot cup of tea, or maybe a coffee, would have been a better choice than iced tea when I'm cold and damp. You live and learn, right?

Mall and Mail!

I'm back at the hotel now, typing while Alan soaks away the day in the onsen. After the disappointment of the Museum of Art, the afternoon was spent hiding from the weather at the Aeon mall, which is supposedly the biggest mall in Shikoku. It was like modern malls anywhere – big, airy, spacious, clean, with a supermarket, food court, toilets, and places to sit. I'm not a huge fan of shopping, but I found enough things to keep me amused until it was time to pop into one of the mall eateries for an early dinner.

I snapped of photo of Alan in a kung fu fighting pose with a Colonel Sanders figure outside the KFC fast food joint. I sent photos of cool samurai hat replicas in a department store to friends back home, and I found some fun stuff to mail home for my granddaughter.

Anyway, her birthday is while I'm away, so I decide to post her gifts today so she will get them in time. Which you'd think would be easy, right? Go to a post office, buy a box, buy some stamps, and mail it. Easy!

Unfortunately, it turned out to be much more complicated than I thought. The nice, friendly staff in the mall post office (yubinkyoku / 〒 / 郵便局) didn't actually know how to send a package to Canada. A letter would have been easy, but a package... not so much so. The first task was relatively easy: find a box the right size to put all the items in. One was successfully selected and paid for. Then began the search for an online shipping form and a price sheet for the different shipping options, followed by a great deal of confusion over how to complete the form. There was a lot of questions and frowning and discussion about whether 'sender's address' was my hotel in Kochi, or my address in Canada. It seemed that the only postal codes which could be put into the system were Japanese ones...

I'd entered the post office a good half an hour before closing time, but despite three of them working on the Great Canadian Mail Challenge there wasn't enough time to complete the task. The staff bowed politely as they showed me the door, and suggested trying again on another day.

Alan and I agree that actually buying a shipping box was quite an achievement, and we're congratulating ourselves on the success of mailing-gifts-to-Canada Stage 1. I'll try a post office walking distance from the hotel for the second attempt instead of taking a tram back here though.

The Yubinkyoku Challenge

Oh, and just a side note: the predicted thunderstorms didn't actually happen and the rain apparently completely stopped around 3pm while I was inside the mall. And do you remember the 'waterproof' shoes I packed? Well perhaps they were waterproof 10 years ago, but they're not anymore!

Water Water Everywhere

Sakawa Sakura

Ki no moto ni
shru mo namasu mo
sakura kana
Beneath the tree, in the soups and salads, cherry blossoms everywhere
(Matsuo Basho)

Today started early (this seems to be becoming a habit) and I was scolded (in a joking way, I think?) by a chef over breakfast when I poured tamari over my bowl of rice. I had no idea why that was frowned upon, but I bowed and apologised anyway. Alan also got into trouble for putting yuzu sauce on his lightly seared bonito, which obviously came as a surprise when there was a dish of bonito-in-yuzu-sauce right there on the buffet. I think the staff just enjoyed the fact that we could understand what they said and were poking fun at us. In a nice way.

Anyhow, we survived breakfast and are heading off to the pretty little village of Sakawa today, hoping for sunshine and sakura blossoms. We're taking the limited express train going to Nakamura from the Kochi JR station, which stops at Sakawa. Here's a little tip – if you take a limited express, you have to buy two train tickets. The first is the basic train ticket, and the second is the extra fare for the faster trains. Make sure you press the limited express button on the ticket vending machines. If you forget, and lots of people do, the conductor on the train will charge you the extra fare and give you the second ticket, so don't panic.

I've read that Sakawa is a pretty little place, with buildings from the Edo period, a 400 year old sake brewery, a geology museum with two woolly mammoth statues (I'm not planning to go here – it's in the opposite direction from where I want to be), and a hillside park with over 17 varieties of sakura trees. There's also Sakawa Bunko Kosha, the oldest western style house in Kochi, and Uemachi Station (which isn't actually a station at all) housing an old wooden railway carriage. Some reviews of Sakawa mention a temple, but I'm not clear on where it is or if it's open to the public or not.

I know Sakawa may not sound like a very exciting place to visit, and it certainly lacks the excitement of big cities like Osaka and Kumamoto. But this is Shikoku. Small, not very touristy, and a place to slow down and smell the roses. Or sakura, as the case may be. The sun's shining, there's the promise of pretty flowers, and I'm looking forward to seeing this quaint old village.

It's only a short walk from the hotel to Kochi train station, and there's fun things to look at on the way. I spot a monkey with a microphone outside what I assume is a karaoke bar. An Anpanman statue sits on a bench next to a busy road, with his nemesis Baikinman and a smaller statue which may or may not be Kokinchan. A little further on I spot Shokupanman and Dokinchan. I'm really not up to date on Anpanman stuff, but I know the creator, Takashi Yanase, was born in Kochi prefecture. There's an Anpanman Museum I would have liked to see, but it's too far away from Kochi City to get to without a car.

Benched

It took the express train about half an hour to get to Sakawa station, and about 10 minutes to walk to the oldest part of the village where I'm now sitting in a cafe with a cup of hot tea and some rice cakes. It used to be the home of Hamaguchi, a local merchant, and it's really old with tatami mats and wood beams. Three ladies (I was going to say 'old', but perhaps they're not really? It's really hard to gauge their ages) are creating amazing 6ft tall ikebana arrangements out of branches cut off trees in the cafe garden. They've obviously been doing this for many, many years. When they saw me watching, they invited me to view a completed arrangement in another room. It was astonishingly beautiful. I told them I've only been studying Ohara Ikebana for 2 years, so I have a lot to learn. They agreed wholeheartedly. Yes, many, many years of study is needed. It looks like I've stumbled upon a hobby which will last a lifetime. My teacher has said she'll apply for my beginner level certificate soon, so at least I'll officially have my foot on the ladder, so to speak. But it will be a l-o-n-g time before I'm allowed to attempt anything this big.

Larger than Life Ikebana

Makino Park

Ok, teatime is over, and I'm heading out into the sunshine to walk up the hill to Makino Park. I'm putting the remaining rice crackers in my bag – you never know when a snack might be required when you're on an adventure!

This is so pretty, even though I'm still a bit too early to see the cherry blossom in full bloom. There's not many people here, the views from the hillside are lovely, and even though the sun is hot and the path is quite steep the walk is enjoyable. I can understand why Makino Park is listed as one of Japan's top 100 cherry blossom viewing locations. It will be splendid next week. But even now I'm going to have a lot of photos of sakura, some of which I hope will be in focus!

It's taken me a good half an hour to reach the open grassy area at the top of the hill, maybe longer, because I keep stopping to admire the flowers and take photos. And, maybe, rest my legs a little lol.

Sunshine Stroll

The summit of Makino Park hill is quite shady, making me worry a bit about mosquitoes and other biting bugs. I don't particularly want to linger up here, nor take the woodland path instead of the paved one on the way back down. I'm a total magnet for biting bugs around the world. Besides, I want to get lunch at a courtyard cafe I passed on the paved route. I could do with a sit down, a bottle of cold green tea, and some onigiri decorated with preserved sakura petals.

Lunch at the cafe place is lovely. After some debate about whether to actually have the onigiri, or perhaps one of the hot oden dishes from the adjacent stall (the rice balls won), the server showed me to a nice shady table in a quiet corner, out of the blazing sun. Unfortunately I'm not the only lifeform looking for a bit of shade. Little biting beasties were hiding under the picnic table and feasted on my ankles while I was preoccupied with my lunch. As usual, Alan hasn't got a single bite, but he's earning forgiveness by buying some red bean mochi for me.

Beauty and The Bugs

It's time to head back down the hill to check out the rest of Sakawa. I take a brief detour to check out a long row of head-height red torii gates leading to an old stone torii gate in front of a small shrine. Some reviews of Sakawa (there's not many of them!) mention visiting the grave of Dr. Makino on Makino Park hill, so maybe this is it? To be honest I'm finding the scarcity of solid information about this place a bit frustrating. I walk through the torii gate tunnel, give a polite bow at the shrine where paper prayers hang on trees and around the necks of stone dragons, and continue on my way.

Torii Time

Near the bottom of the hill, there's a temple where I can hear chanting and drums. This might be Jodaiji or Seigenji temple, but I'm not sure. Everyone else here is just walking by without a second glance at the mossy stone steps or the garden walls, leading me to believe it's either not open to tourists or isn't in fact a place with *'one of the finest temple gardens in Kochi'*. Alan's going to take a look anyway, and I feel a bit uncomfortable watching him over the garden wall as he wanders out of sight.

He's back, and isn't particularly overwhelmed by the beauty of what he saw in the grounds, so I remain unsure of what this temple is. Maybe even the 'finest temple gardens' in Kochi don't look impressive this early in the spring?

More Makino!

The walk back to the village takes me by a large sake warehouse, which presumably belongs to Tsukasabotan Brewery, and I arrive at the oldest wooden western style building in Kochi. Sakawa Bunko Kosha was built in 1886 in the style of a house from the Meiji era and was the Sakawa police station until being moved to a side street in 2010. It's painted white, has 2 stories, pillars, shutters, and a balcony above the front door. There's not much to see inside, but outside is a gorgeous flower arrangement in the shape of a life-size ball gown, perfect for me to stand behind for a photo. It must have taken hours to create it out of a whole load of yellow, orange and cream flowers.

Next door is home to an old wooden railway carriage, where Alan takes a photo of me half-hidden behind the carriage's open door. We do this in memory of my dad, whose love of railways often resulted in family photos where trains were always in focus, but me not so much so.

Fashionably Floral

Our final stop before leaving Sakawa is a tourism office dedicated to (want to have a guess?)... Dr. Makino! He was actually born in Sakawa, and raised by his grandmother after both his parents passed away. He left at the age of 17 to study in Tokyo, and died at the age of 94 in Oizumi (about an hour away from Tokyo). The tourist office is a replica of the house he grew up in, and I chat with the guide about all kinds of things including Makino, my snow-covered garden back home, and the beauty of sakura, and we share pictures of our cats. She's making a documentary about Dr. Makino and asks if Alan and I would record something for the countdown of the documentary's release. She shows us earlier ones of tourists and locals holding a number, and I say 'sure'. We sit on the edge of the floor of Dr. Makino's childhood home, hold up a number, and Alan says something along the lines of 'coming soon'. The tourist guide is delighted, and gives us both a roll of floral washi tape with 'Sakawa' written on it as thanks. I'll be using it to stick photos of floral arrangements in my ikebana scrap book when I get home.

Sakawa on Tape

I've had a lovely day in Sakawa, arriving back in Kochi in time to walk to a post office for a second attempt at mailing a package back home. Long story short, it's taken me 40 minutes (!) to wade through all the on-line forms with the postal staff, and finally work out how to send the box from Kochi to Ottawa. Every item being sent has to be categorised according to specific rules, and it's taken the staff a long time, and a lot of discussion and deep thinking, to work out how to label a small plastic Pikachu Pokémon.

Closing time has arrived before the task is completed. I've been escorted out of the door and showered with promises that the box will be labelled, sealed and mailed in my absence. Goodness knows when it will get there!

(Spoiler alert – it took 3 days).

How to Post a Pokémon

Ekin, more Ekin, and Ryoma

Harusame ya
Monogatariyuku
Mino to kasa
Gentle spring rain, walking lost in conversation, straw cloak and umbrella
(Yosa Buson)

After yesterday's glorious sunshine the rain has returned, and we're on the hunt for indoor activities. Preferably ones which are actually open. Tomorrow is Sunday market day, with a visit to the castle in the afternoon. On Monday we have tickets for a special train ride to Kubokawa, and, whatever the weather, we're going to the beach on Tuesday. So that leaves today wide open. I think it's time for a trip out of the city centre in search of arts and culture, and I don't mean returning to the Kochi Museum of Art to see if they'll let us in this time lol.

So... We're on a local train heading east to Akaoka, looking for a museum of Ekin screen paintings. Sounds like fun, right? Oh, what? You don't know what an Ekin painting is? To be honest, neither did I until I was researching things to do in Kochi. A quick Google search for Ekin will take you to pages about a Hong Kong actor, but he's not the guy we're checking out today. We're much more interested in Hirose Kinzo, the Japanese artist from the Edo period, right? More details to come! (Drum roll to create a feeling of suspense).

Drum Roll

The 40 minute train ride has brought me to what looks like a ghost town. Alan and I are the only people who got off the train here (did I mention today is Saturday?) on this dark, rainy day. The only figures to be seen are large plastic cartoon figures in a long display case at the station, representing the mascots of local towns and villages. The few shops I walk by are closed, there's no cafes to be seen, and there's not even a Family Mart to buy snacks. It's totally dead. I recall reading someone's blog referring to Akaoka as 'the eerily quiet old quarter', and now I understand what he meant! I'm beginning to suspect the plastic mascots might be the only 'people' I actually encounter in Akaoka! I'm assuming the rather sinister-looking one with a paintbrush in his hand is Ekin. Another looks like Tora-San with his suitcase – I visited his museum in Shibamata when I was there a few years ago.

Not Real People, But...

Ekin Museum

The Ekin museum, tucked up a side street next to an old theatre, looks like a warehouse. Inside I'm greeted by a lady who asks if I can speak Japanese. 'Only a little' I reply, and Alan nods in confirmation. So, as often happens, I'm then bombarded with a whole ton of rapidly spoken complicated Japanese sentences, out of which I try to pick the important information. On this occasion the only bits which I understand are 'pick up a lantern, go upstairs, watch a movie'. OK! I can do that!

The movie has shed some light on who Ekin was, and here's the summary of what I remember:

Ekin was born in Kochi (then known as Tosa) in 1812. His mother was a hairdresser, although some say he was born into a family of merchants, and some say his adopted father was a doctor. At the age of 17 he travelled to Edo (Tokyo) to study under prestigious artists of the time, Maemura Tōwa and Kano Masunobu. He changed his name to Hayashi Toi, and at the age of twenty returned home to become the personal artist of Tosa's chief retainer. Unfortunately he was accused of plagiarism and lost his job, his home in Kochi castle and his reputation as a painter. Did he really forge some works by Kano Tan'yu? There's some debate about that. I think the movie said he was asked to copy a painting, and then a signature was added to it by an enemy, turning a 'copy' into a 'forgery' or something like that. Information on the following 10 years seems to be a bit murky, but he might have changed his name numerous times, somehow eventually purchasing the Hirose surname from a town doctor. No, I don't understand that either. Anyway, his aunt eventually helped him settle in Akaoka in Kōnan, where he called himself Town Painter Kinzō. His studio was a sake brewery, and there are some suggestions that he 'liked to drink'. The locals called him Ekin, which is an abbreviation of the Japanese words for 'Painter Kinzō'. They asked him to create paintings on storyboards, lanterns and kites for them. He became well known for his often gruesome paintings based on folk tales on folding screens (shibai-e byoubu), which are claimed to contain 'beautifully frightening energy'. They're supposed to be viewed by candlelight, and in July every year his folding screens are placed in the streets of Akaoka for a night festival illuminated with lanterns.

And now you know as much as I do about Ekin.

Anyway, now I'm standing in a dimly lit room, holding my battery operated paper lantern towards replicas of some of Ekin's paintings, under the watchful gaze of a member of staff. No flash photography is allowed, even though the paintings aren't 'real'. I suppose it's to preserve the eerie atmosphere as much as anything else. Some of the painted screens tell an entire story, others just fragments. The images are quite graphic, depicting folk tales involving murder, beheadings, ghosts, spurting blood, and occasional male genitalia. I love it. Ekin used a lot (and I mean a LOT) of blood red in his artwork, which villagers believed would protect them from bad luck and evil spirits.

The guide directs me to a small hole in the wall where I can peep at an original, genuine Ekin painting in an adjacent room. Cool eh?

The next room in this small museum has sketches and paintings (no photography allowed), one of which makes Alan laugh out loud. What looks at first glance to be some sort of orgy is actually a village farting contest, and there are lots of exposed bottoms being closely scrutinised by what I assume are the contest judges. So, not porn, just Edo period humour. And no, I'm not going to draw a picture of that for you!

Ekin by Lantern Light

ACTLand

The next stop on our day of high art and culture is ACTland, one train station away from Akaoka. I think the first thing I'll do when I get to Noichi is hunt for food. Apart from some rice crackers I bought in Sakawa yesterday neither Alan nor I have any snacks in our bags, and it's been a long time since breakfast! A hot cup of tea would also be really, really nice, but I suspect we'll be sitting in a convenience store drinking tea from a bottle and eating onigiri.

Konbini Lunch

When I first saw a brochure for ACTland I had visions of something like Tohei film studio park near Kyoto, because, you know, 'act' land? Turns out ACT stands for Art, Culture and Technology, and ACTland was created because 'It's essential for humanity to become familiar with the arts, refine culture, and develop science and technology'. The museum has eight different mini-museums, including a container gallery with 'artefacts and relics that cannot be found elsewhere'. I really hope it's going to be worth the cold damp 15 minute walk from the train station.

I've walked through the empty outdoor playground (it's raining – there's probably kids playing here on a sunny day), past a ferris wheel powered by a bicycle, and bought tickets for all eight museums. It's definitely not cheap, but I figure there's not much point coming here and then not seeing everything ACTland has to offer. I'm currently standing in the world celebrity waxworks museum, and it's kinda creepy. There's lots of very realistic figures of old guys in military uniforms (and I mean 'lots'), some of which are apparently fixated on a terrible waxwork of Marilyn Monroe in a display opposite them. There's some equally bad waxworks of western political figures, a scary one of Cleopatra, and one of Ghandi sitting in front of a painting of the Taj Mahal. I don't want to linger in here. I feel like all the wax eyes are following me.

So, moving on, guess where I am now? I'm in... the Ekin Art Gallery! Yes, more Ekin art. There's better lighting than in the Ekin museum in Akaoka, but I sort of miss the eerie atmosphere of the previous place. This much larger gallery has some lots-of-blood paintings (replicas, I assume?), but there's also works from his 'Portraits of Beauty' and 'Painting of Customs' series, and some Chinese-influenced Kano-style folding screens. Additional paintings by disciples who were heavily influenced by Ekin are also on display. I think if I just wanted to see paintings by Ekin I'd go to the dimly lit warehouse in Akaoka instead of coming here. It's much more atmospheric, although a lot smaller.

I've now moved on to the 'big attraction' here in ACTland – the Ryoma History Museum. Ryoma Sakamoto is one of the big political heroes of Kochi, not to be confused with Ryoma Takebayashi, a 39 year old cartoon character reincarnated as an 8 year old boy who lives in a world inhabited by slime monsters.

I'm intrigued by the flyer for this museum, and I'm not quite sure what to expect. It says 'The 33 years of life in which Sakamoto Ryoma fled like the wind is recreated in the Ryoma Theatre'. There's 27 historical scenes over 120 wax dolls, and added effects of light and sound 'in a full theatrical atmosphere'. There's also a Ryoma Document Hall exhibiting the 'Hokushinitto-ryu Certificate of the Art of War of a Long Handled Sword'. The info sheet also states that 'The content of the attractions is sufficient', whatever that means.

So, what is this Ryoma theatre museum? Well, it's basically lots of scenes with waxworks and sound effects, telling the life story of a lowly samurai who was born in Kochi in 1836, grew up to be a political activist, was instrumental in bringing about the Meiji restoration, and was assassinated in 1867 at the age of 31. Or at the age of 33, depending on where you get your information from. Thank goodness for the thick handout with scene-by-scene information printed in English! I would be totally lost without it. It seems to take an eternity to walk around, but I linger at intriguing places such as where Ryoma's wife saves him from being murdered when she ran upstairs to warn him 'without changing out of her bathing clothes', and the really sad part where his eldest sister kills herself. It's a good place to learn about local political history, but you probably need an attention span longer than mine to really appreciate it. But if you like history and waxworks it's a very impressive museum and you should visit if you're in the area.

Here's a fun fact I *didn't* learn at the museum. Asteroid 2835 Ryoma was discovered in November 1982 by an amateur Japanese astronomer living in Kochi and named after Ryoma Sakamoto.

So now onto something I actually find interesting: Kuma's Container Gallery. I'm standing under a large red tarpaulin roof viewing shipping containers which have one side removed with pieces of 'simple work with no glamour' art made out of metal, glass, wood and plastic displayed inside. Fun fun fun! And all a bit strange, to be honest. I'm most intrigued by a large metal globe with an open 'mouth' containing large rusty scissors. It's like something out of a science fiction movie, and I love it.

I'm afraid I can't tell you much about the artist, other than what I saw on the museum website. Searches for Kuma, also known as Katsuyuki Shinohara, turn up results for a movie director of the same name but I don't think it's the same person. There's some intriguing (if a bit confusing) information about the artist on the ACTland website, but I've not been able to find much about him anywhere else. According to the museum website, Katsuyuki Shinohara wrote an essay called 'Life is a Diamond,' and was 'active in the media as The Bear of the Gadgets'. He's said to have a 'unique creative style that transcends borders, such as Manhattan and Mongolia, and marks the earth'. Apparently his works have been praised for their 'stateless power and overwhelming presence'.

Anyway... the artwork here is intriguing. I've already mentioned the scissor-mouth globe, but there's lots more to see. Blobs of illuminated glass. Bodies made out of wire. Sheets of metal curved into shapes. It's fun.

There's No Real Actors in ACTland

I'm about ready to leave ACTland, but Alan wants to see the remaining museums so I'm sitting on a chair in the World Classic Car Museum while he wanders around. These full-size real vehicles are a bit more interesting than contents of the World Model Car Museum, which had illuminated display cabinets containing over 3,000 tiny cars, many of which to my untrained eye looked identical. The Bonnet Bus Museum had, pretty much as one would expect, some old buses, which didn't get me terribly excited. But I quite enjoyed the gallery of metal art – this is apparently the only museum in the world with about 300 works of art by Francis Kwatei Nee-Owoo from Ghana. Apparently he's been friends with the head of ACTland for over 20 years, which is why his art is here, I suppose. The metalwork art is very 'African', and to be honest wasn't what I was expecting to find in a museum in Kochi, but maybe that's part of the purpose of the ACT museum? The ACTland brochure says the art gallery has 'special effects and LED lighting technology… which is rarely found in other art museums. Softly lighting each of Nee-Owoo's works with LED produces a magical atmosphere'. I have to admit that the 'magical atmosphere' was kinda lost on me, but it's been a very long day.

Well Lit Art

As we leave ACTland I mention to Alan that one of the Shikoku-88 pilgrimage temples is a 15 minute walk away, but neither of us can muster enough energy or enthusiasm to make it happen. We're cold, wet from the rain, tired, and both limping quite badly at this point. It's been an interesting day, but we just want to go back to Kochi. We stagger to the train station, pausing for a cup of hot tea in a Mister Donut along the way, then we sit in the damp air for 45 minutes waiting for the next train. There's a couple of bedraggled pilgrims on the opposite platform, looking quite cold and tired. They're Caucasian, so they probably had a long journey from a foreign land to freeze their rain-soaked butts off in Shikoku. I think sometimes an umbrella might be more useful than a walking stick.

You Can't Use a Walking Stick as an Umbrella

The train finally arrives, and I sigh as I sink into my seat for the ride back to Kochi. It's been a long, cold, damp day, and it's nice to be sitting somewhere warm and dry.

Dinner plans for tonight include a short tram ride to a Coco Curry restaurant close to the hotel for delicious, inexpensive food and a large beer. You can't go wrong with a Japanese curry at the end of a rainy day.

Sunday Market, Music and A Castle

Harusame ya
Kasa sashite miru
Ezoshiya
Spring rain, browsing under an umbrella at the picture bookstore
(Masaoka Shiki)

It's Sunday, so it must be Sunday Market Day! I'm up bright and early as usual, long before breakfast opens at 6:30, giving me lots of time to plan today's activities in the spring rain. Yes, it's another wet day in Kochi. Armed with my Family Mart umbrella, it's time to shop like a local, celebrate like a local (more about that later!), eat like a local, and visit the castle like a total tourist.

Kochi Sunday Market has been held in the same location for over 300 years. It stretches for over a km along the road I walked along when I went to the castle, ending at the Otemon gate. It opens at 5am (5:30am during the cooler months of the year). I've seen varying reports on how many vendors sell their goods at the market, ranging from 300 to 500. Perhaps it depends on the season and the weather.

The market is bustling even on this grey day. Umbrellas make navigating between the two rows of stalls challenging, but being much taller than most of the locals seems to give me a slight advantage as long as I remember to duck when I'm near a tarpaulin. I'm not sure 300 venders have turned up today, but the promised 'must see' stalls are here. There's lots of locally grown produce, with numerous vendors displaying fragrant citrus fruits, and some selling freshly cut flowers. I buy myself a bunch of bananas, which I suspect are not local. Okinawa grows bananas, so maybe they're from there? Not that I really care. I just want a banana!

Unlike markets I've been to in big cities, there's no 'tourist tack' here today. No solar powered bobble head geisha dolls, no Pokémon toys, no postcards. It's a local market for local folks.

As I wander around, I become aware that someone is following me. Every time I stop I can see him out of the corner of my eye. He comes closer when I linger at a stall selling pickles, so I turn to him and smile. He smiles back and asks where I'm from. Ottawa. He looks blankly at me, so I try again. Canada. That makes him happy – he's got a friend in Vancouver! He thinks Canadians are very nice people. He asks again where I live, so I try 'Near Toronto'. Yes! He knows where Toronto is. It's odd how everyone seems to know the capital city of our province, but not the capital city of the entire country. Which is Ottawa, in case you're wondering lol.

There's lines forming in front of fast food vendors as people wait to buy yakitori (chicken skewers) or sweet potato tempura, but it's a very popular strawberry stall which catches my eye. The aroma is incredible, and I can't help but join the line of people waiting to buy a strawberry mochi (a fresh strawberry encased in chewy pounded rice dough) in a square plastic box from the vendor's fridge.

Sweet Dreams are Made of These

It's the most expensive strawberry I will ever buy, but it's totally worth it. Soft, sweet, fragrant. It's the kind of thing poems should be written about. Alan buys me a bunch of tiny narcissus to brighten our sombre hotel room. I would have also loved some cherry blossoms, but had to concede that the branches were much too big to actually fit in the space available.

But I digress. I've read that handmade knives are sold at the market, and I want to check them out. I'm also on the hunt for some new ikebana scissors, and I'm delighted to find a couple of pairs that I really like. They're expensive, and I'll have to mail them home, but I'll get lots of use out of them. I believe I've finally mastered the art of sending packages to Canada, and I'm confident that it will all go without a hitch. (It did!)

Marvelous Market

Makino and Music!

After a quick detour to put the flowers in an empty sake bottle back at the hotel, I'm heading to the tourist information office plaza to see what an 'event happening here' sign is all about. Today is a brand new holiday in Shikoku: Makino Botanical Day. I ask in the tourist info office what's going on, and she says the fenced off area is free to enter, and there will be a performance of Yosakoi starting shortly. Sounds like fun!

My temperature is scanned at the marquee entrance and declared to be acceptable, and I enter the event grounds. There's little stalls selling floral knickknacks, some craft tables for the kids, a row of food trucks, and a big stage with chairs in front. I look around for Alan and see he's being held captive by a lady holding a book about Dr. Makino and speaking to him in a very excited way while waving the book around. Should I go rescue him? Nah. Maybe he's learning something useful.

As it turns out, he wasn't.

I've sat down on one of the chairs, accepted a naruko (wooden clapper) given to me by a guide, and I'm waiting for the performance to start. I saw Yosakoi dancers on the videos at the Yosakoi Centre a couple of days ago, so I'm excited to see it in real life!

Yosakoi Rising Star

This is great! The dance troupe definitely has a 'Shikoku country folk' thing going on, dressed in white shirts with blue spots, long pants, dark blue aprons, and beige flat caps. The dancers range in age from someone in their 60's down to a child who is probably around five. She's the star of the show even though she's not sure what any of the dance moves are. As the music plays and the dancers dance, a couple of guys take turns waving around a HUGE flag off to the side. The fabric is probably over 24ft long, but it's hard to gauge the true size as it waves around. This is flag waving on a truly impressive scale! Finding this free event was definitely a stroke of good luck.

Kochi castle

Kochi castle is the main reason why I came to Kochi, so after a quick plate of fried noodles I'm looking forward to an afternoon of exploring and taking photos in the not-as-rainy-as-it-was-when-I-first-arrived weather. Obviously I'd been hoping for clear cerulean blue skies, happy chirping birds and masses of sakura blooms, but I'll settle for intermittent showers under a grey sky at this point.

Kochi castle was built in the early 1600's on Otokayama hill as a replacement for a smaller castle in a nearby town. There's a number of confusing stories about who built it, but as far as I can work out Katsutoya Yamauchi, the first Lord of Tosa, was the guy. He was a vassal of the feudal lord Toyotomi Hideyoshi, but after receiving a secret message from his wife he switched allegiances mid-battle, helping to secure a win for the Tokugawa shogunate. As a result, his family ruled Tosa (Kochi) for nearly 300 years.

A fire destroyed most of the castle in 1727, and reconstructed was completed in 1753. It survived the post-meiji era orders to destroy feudal castles and was also undamaged during World War II. Renovations were done in 1900's, and the castle was designated a 'Historical Site' with 15 'National Cultural Assets' buildings.

Before heading to the castle itself I make a stop at the castle museum to see various artifacts like pottery, cool helmets, masks and swords. The best part of the museum is actually the huge picture window with a fantastic view of the castle. The white walls and ornate roof look quite dramatic despite the grey skies.

I'm happy to linger here a moment, enjoying the view while Alan is making a free 'woodcut' picture using plastic stamps provided by the museum. I don't think it's his best artwork to be honest, but he's having fun.

Stamped

I enter the castle grounds, pose briefly under the otemon (impressive wooden gateway) for a photo shoot without my umbrella, then begin the climb up the multitude of stone steps leading to the castle itself. I'm not suffering from the overwhelming jet-lag fatigue I had the first time I visited the castle and make it to the top without drama, but I have to admit it's a bit of a hike! There's a few damp sakura asking to be photographed on the way up, so I stop from time to time to take shots of the pretty flowers.

Before entering the castle I buy my ticket at a vending machine, put my shoes in a locker, hand my ticket in at the booth, and shortly afterwards duck under the first low beam of the day. Following the arrows to make sure I don't deviate from the 'recommended' route, I walk past display cases with historical artifacts, and admire a small model of the castle and surrounding areas in the 17th century. With a deep sigh I approach the first of numerous sets of stairs which will take me to the top of the castle. I'm not a fan of castle stairs. The people ahead of me are climbing them very slowly, which I know from experience is the only safe way to get up steep, slippery, ladder-like constructions. I often draw myself as someone small and cute, but in reality I'm quite tall, giving me lots of opportunities to bump my head on low beams.

The view from the top of the castle keep is lovely. There's Shachihoko on the rooftop. These half-fish-half-dragon decorations originated in China but became popular in Japan in the 1400's. They're supposed to channel water onto rooftops to reduce the risk of fire, but considering that most Japanese castles have burnt down at least once I don't know how successful they are at that.

The Castle of Kochi

Looking down from the top of the keep, I can see people milling around in the courtyard, which is surrounded by thick stone walls. It's stopped raining, and while I wouldn't describe the skies as clear it's good enough for me to see the hills surrounding Kochi City. The views definitely make the climb worthwhile this time, with no need for facetious comments about bluebirds or people bursting into song. It probably looks even better on a sunny day.

On the way back down I'm taking time to admire more displays of old samurai armour and helmets, check out some swords, and take a few calming breaths between each flight of stairs. Slippery socks and shiny wood are even scarier on the way back down than they were on the way up.

I think navigating my way through the castle without injuring myself deserves a hot cup of tea!

Dancing and Dinner

Hirome market, best known for flamed hunks of fish, turns out to be a nice place for a hot pot of oolong tea served with mugwort dango. Yes, mugwort. Sounds yummy eh? It's a perennial plant, but at its best about the same time the cherry blossoms are blooming. The muddy-green coloured squishy pounded rice balls are the perfect afternoon treat with a hot cuppa in a sweets café tucked away in the fishy market.

Mugwort for Muggles

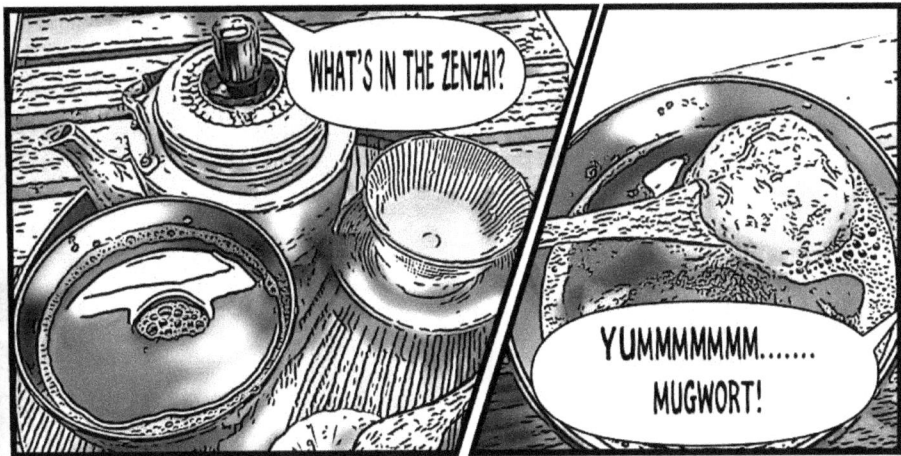

Dance Off!

After a bit of wandering around the shops (I picked up some anime music CDs to take home as a gift) I'm heading somewhere for dinner, but not before I see the outcome of a dance off taking place in front of a department store. It's better than anything I've seen on America's Got Talent! Real high energy 'in your face' dancing, both by solo dancers and tag-teams of 2. I think my favourites so far are a tiny girl dressed in black wearing a cool hat, and a buff guy dancing to 'I'm every woman'.

Dinner tonight is at a Korean BBQ restaurant. We've successfully ordered food, and managed to cook it with the assistance of the waiters, but to be honest we have no clue what we're doing. I'm happy with my choice of tofu hotpot, but Alan is struggling a bit making sure his chicken is cooked enough to not give him food poisoning. I guess we'll find out soon how successful he is.

(Spoiler alert: He was fine.)

Hotpots

Train and Temple Day

Kasha sugite
Kemuri uzumaku
Wakaba kana
The train passes in a whirl of smoke – young leaves
(Masaoka Shiki)

This morning I've taken a tram down to the Horikawa canal area and am having a romantic stroll with the love of my life under the cherry blossom trees. Alan and I are celebrating the anniversary of our wedding on a rainy day in England 'a few' years ago. We're alone here except for a man taking photos of the flowers. He's fascinating to watch, bowing rapidly and repeatedly before each shot. He obviously takes both his spiritual connection with nature and his photography a lot more seriously than I do. I have no doubt that his photos will be better than mine. Maybe because of the bowing, but probably because he has an enormous camera mounted on a tripod.

Bow, Rise, Repeat

It's a beautiful morning for a walk. The sun is shining, but it's not too hot. The sakura are in full bloom, lining both edges of the pathway along the water's edge. A gentle breeze wafts petals into my hair and onto my beloved's baseball cap. Ah, l'amour.

When we lovebirds have tired of walking, we take a tram to the JR railway station, narrowly avoiding getting on one going in the wrong direction. We're both struggling a bit cognitively today, but I'm sure a hot cup of tea and a red bean filled pastry at the station bakery will sort us out.

Happy Anniversary!

Tosa no Yoakeno Monogatari

Today we're taking a ride on a special train trip to Kubokawa, which I reserved on-line before leaving home. It's a lovely sunny day, perfect for just sitting on a train for a couple of hours watching the scenery of Kochi drift by. Launched in 2020, the Shikoku Tosa no Yoakeno Monogatari (tale of the dawn of an era) luxury heritage two-car train promises 'majestic views of the countryside and the sparkling Pacific Ocean, and you can savour the flavours of Kochi as you travel through space and time'. The train runs along the route which Ryoma Sakamoto (you remember him from the ACTland museum, right?) took when fleeing from opponents at the end of the Edo period. I'm seated in the futuristic sorafune (sky ship) carriage, with sparkly stars on a black ceiling, golden pillars, and white swivel chairs. It's a 'nod to Ryoma's dreams for the future of Japan'. It's perfect for a wedding anniversary, but for me probably too expensive for a 'normal' holiday experience.

And we're off! The train is moving really slowly, accentuating the sideways slope of the railway tracks. There's a commentary, presumably about Ryoma, but it's in Japanese and it's too much effort to concentrate on picking up familiar words so I just let it drift over me while I admire the rugged countryside gently sliding by.

Lunch is served, beautifully presented in a hexagonal bento box, with descriptions of the food printed on a pretty menu. When the attendant has moved into the other carriage I quietly swap some very fishy items in my bento box with fruits and vegetables from Alan's. We're both happy with this arrangement.

I hadn't realised before, but we have a job to do as guests on this special train. We are required to wave like royalty to people as we pass. The attendants take it very seriously and tell us where and when. 'Please wave to people on our left. Please wave to people on our right. Please wave to people on both sides. Please wave to the people standing on a balcony with flags. Please wave to the lady dancing on the platform in our honour. Please wave to the lady holding the sign saying 'welcome'.' Honestly this is a big responsibility. Oh look: there's two women running alongside the train with flags. I have to stop writing and wave. And... oh wait... There's some in a parking lot. I'll have to come back to this later. Unless my arm is too tired from all this waving. Oh! That lady is dressed like a bottle of beer! I give her an extra big wave as I take a quick sip from my own beer bottle.

Well that was lovely. A bit weird, but lovely. We've arrived in Kubokawa and I'm resisting the urge to wave at people sitting in parked cars or waiting to cross the road. I'm heading off to one of the 88 temples, but I can't remember which one right now. (It's number 37!) But first, I have to wait for Alan to reappear. One of the other passengers left his bag on the train, so Alan has run after him so they can be reunited.

Training to be a Professional Waver

Iwamotoji

It's a short walk from the train station to Iwamotoji, temple 37 of the 88 temple pilgrimage. The primary deity of this temple is Amida Nyora (a pure kingdom Buddha) and it's a place to be happy and enjoy life. It's the home of five deities (most temples just worship one), but that's not what makes this place unique. When the main hall was rebuilt in 1978, a contest was organised to create artwork for the ceiling, and contemporary artists helped to design the temple grounds. Motivational messages like 'touch the sky' and 'feel the ohenro 37' are written on the steps leading into the complex, leading to the least scary dragon I've ever seen spouting water into a tsukubai (ceremonial wash basin).

There's a number of small shrines in the gravel courtyard, along with a bronze statue of Kukai / Kobo Daishi. If you remember, I mentioned him way back at the beginning of the book. He's the guy who began the whole Shikoku-pilgrimage thing. I'm sure there's at least one statue of him at each of the 88 temples on the trail. A ramshackle little garden has large white plastic globes at the edge, which I assume glow when it gets dark. A large statue of Kannon holds a small child, and statues of Fudu Myoo, Jizo, Amida and Yakushi complete the set of five deities.

A couple of pilgrims were saying their mantras in front of the main hall, but now that they've moved on I can see inside and it was worth the wait. The ceiling is covered in small square paintings in every style imaginable. There's an image of a Noh mask next to a simple painting of a white cat. I see flowers, a tiger, trees, landscapes, portraits, a starry sky. Buddha, cranes, more cats. There's over 600 images, and it's lovely. I've heard there's one of Marilyn Monroe, but I can't see her from where I'm standing. (After returning home I spot Marilyn on one of Alan's photos of the ceiling, along with ones of R2D2 and C3PO! I don't know whether it was pure luck on his part or if he actually knew where to look.)

The temple has a fun, relaxed, 'hippy' kind of feeling. Apparently pilgrims can reserve a room here for the night or camp in the grounds, with the option of sitting in the river to meditate before heading to the rooftop sauna. I think I'll give that a miss.

I get my temple 37 pilgrimage calligraphy page completed at the office, then it's time to head back to the station to take a slow (3 hours, but cheap) train home.

Fun Temple 37

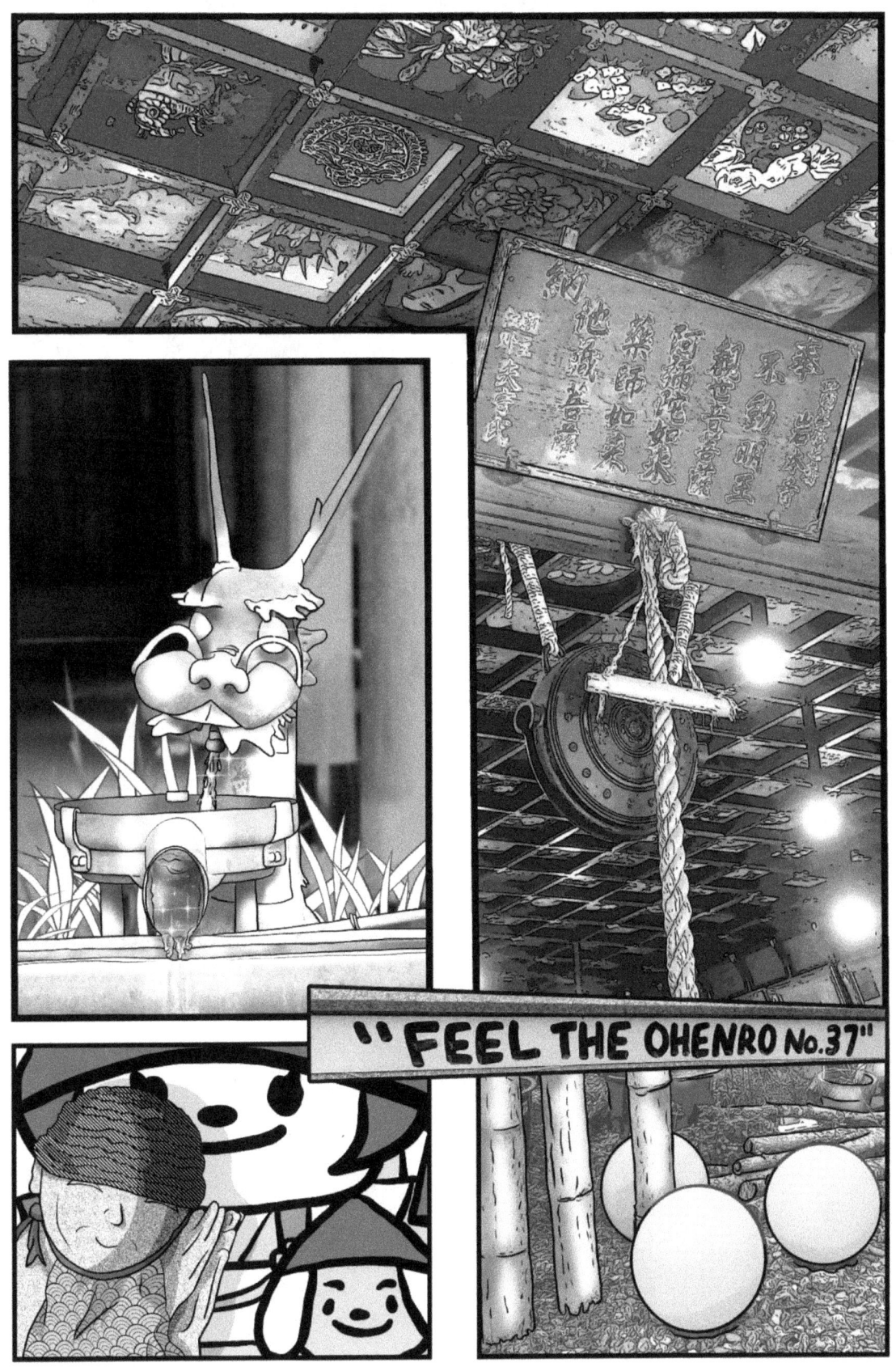

Just a quick note before bed – I had my first ever yuzu beer with dinner tonight, and it was delicious! The perfect accompaniment to my French fries (I can't eat rice absolutely every meal!), deep fried seaweed, pickled eggplant, chilled edamame, and tempura vegetables. Not the healthiest meal I've ever had, but I'm making no apologies.

Cheers!

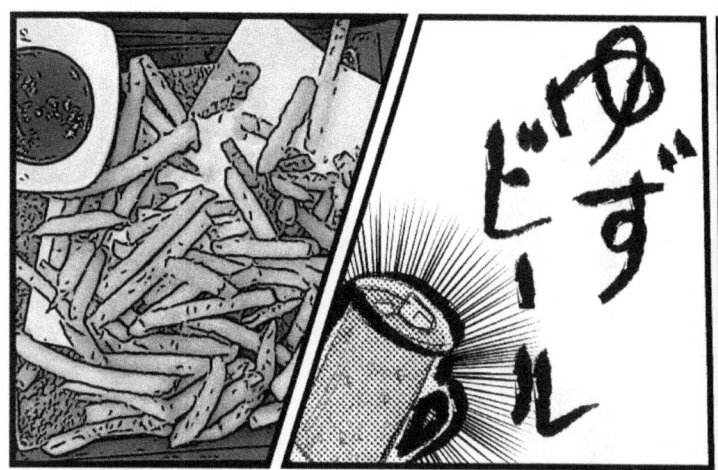

Beach Day

Sunahama ni
Aashiato nagaki
Haruhi kana
On the sandy beach a long line of footsteps, the spring day
(Masaoka Shiki)

A trip to Katsurahama beach on the MyYu bus was postponed a couple of times due to inclement weather, so today's my last chance to go before moving on to Matsuyama. Fortunately it's a sunny day. Breezy, not too hot. Sounds just about perfect. Swimming is prohibited at Katsurahma due to very strong currents, so I don't need to pack a swimsuit before walking to the tourist info plaza. It would be a shorter walk to the MyYu bus stop at Harimayabashi, but I suspect it's easier to get a seat where the bus starts its journey.

I was right! By the time we left the plaza bus stop all the seats were full, and a couple of people were standing. More people will be squishing on board at Harimayabashi.

Busy Bus-y

Sekkeiji

When we arrived at Katsurahama bus stop, Alan and I jumped onto a conveniently timed local bus and headed up into the village to visit Sekkeiji, temple #33 of the Shikoku 88 pilgrimage temples. It's a pleasant place, but there's nothing 'exciting' to report, so it's a bit of a disappointment. There were signs saying pilgrims must not bong the big temple bell to announce their arrival. Maybe that's because this is a Zen Buddhist temple? Or maybe the people living nearby don't like the noise? Perhaps the bell is old and fragile. I dunno.

No Bonging

I'm happy for the visit here to be a brief one, making a quick trip to the bathroom (the toilet seat is cold, which is a lot more common in Shikoku that anywhere else I've been in Japan) then paying 300 yen to have my pilgrimage book stamped and signed. The beauty of the calligraphy makes up for the unmemorable temple.

I might as well give you a bit of history since I don't have much else to say about this place. Chosokabe Motochika, born in Oto castle as the son of a vassal in the late 1500's, was a fearsome samurai. He was a huge fan of burning down temples, but he's best known for playing a major role in unifying all of Shikoku before handing most of it over to the Honshu warlord Toyotomi Hideyoshi in 1584. When his son died in Hideyoshi's battle to conquer Kyushu, Chosokabe chose Sekkeiji to be his ancestral temple and buried his son's ashes here. Chosokabe's own grave is a 20 minute walk away but I'm not going to see it.

I'm going to go for a bit of a wander around the area before looking for a bus stop, because there's no bus due for quite a while and it's a shame to stand around doing nothing.

So now, after checking out another local temple (not one of the 88 temples), I'm standing around doing nothing anyway at what I hope is a bus stop. Google is insisting it's here at a crossroads but is a bit vague about the actual location, or which of the intersecting roads leads back down to the beach area. Alan's found a rusty pole embedded in the pavement, which might be what we're looking for? An old man walks by, and looks astonished when I ask him 'is this a bus stop?'. He looks at the pole as if he's never seen it before, and after some deep thought declares that yes, it is indeed a bus stop. He continues to gaze at it for a while before shrugging and shuffling on his way. The online timetable says the bus should arrive at 11:56. Japanese public transport is very punctual, and it's now 11:58 so I'm getting a little anxious. I breathe a sigh of relief when it eventually appears and stops in front of the rusty pole. It really is a bus stop. Hurray!

Pole-ish Revelations

Katsurahama Beach

After lunch at the beach food court I'm writing this on my phone, sitting on pebbles watching waves gently break on large rocks at the water's edge. It's finally warmed up enough for me to take off my hoody. The breeze coming in from the ocean is very welcome as the sun beats down, and I'm pretty sure I've got a sunburn on my nose. Before settling down on the warm beach, Alan and I took a romantic stroll along the wooden boardwalk to the end of the sand, walked over an arched bridge, and climbed to the blustery hilltop lookout. The view was lovely. I stopped briefly at a tiny vermillion shrine on the way back down and took a photo of Alan in front of a whale made from flowers next to the boardwalk. It marks the entrance to an aquarium, but I didn't want to go in.

Another place I don't intend to visit is the Ryoma Museum at the top of the hill. I think I already know enough about him and his merry band of men. I did, however, stop at the impressively large statue of the man himself as he gazes over the ocean from the hilltop.

After a relaxing day I think the plan now is to get a yuzu sherbet back at the food court then take the MyYu bus back home. Alan is going to head to the castle to take some photos in the late afternoon sunshine while I do some laundry. Dinner plans will probably involve sake, chilled tofu, vegetable tempura, edamame and pickles for me, with fish, fish, fish and fish for Alan lol. It's been a beautiful busy beachy MyYu bus day.

Matsuyama, Ehime

henro shite
haiku no kuni e
iri ni keri
On my pilgrimage I walk into haiku country
(Shuji Niwano)

After a gentle post-breakfast stroll, a large chunk of today has been spent travelling from Kochi to Matsuyama for the second part of my trip. I boarded a JR coach at Hirayama Bashi, and was pleasantly surprised to discover that it was very comfortable. When I bought the ticket online before leaving Canada I worried that it would be small and cramped, but decided to travel by coach anyway because it's much cheaper and faster than doing the journey by train. The 2 hours and 45 minutes passed fairly quickly, and I lost count of the number of long tunnels passing through the mountains before the road eventually ran along the coastline. I enjoyed the ride; it was actually quite nice to just sit for a while and do nothing except gaze out of the window at the rugged landscape. FYI the coach bathroom was worthy of being in a nice hotel!

Kochi prefecture has been left behind, and I'm now in Ehime. It's divided into 3 regions: Nanyo, Chyuo and Toyo. Nanyo, in the south, is best known for its old villages, and I'll be travelling to Uchiko to check one of these out. The central region of Chyuo is home to the capital city, Matsuyama, which will be my base for the next few days. The eastern section, Toyo, is connected by a series of bridges to 6 islands in the Seto Inland Sea, which are popular with hikers and cyclists in the warmer months of the year. I'll be heading up to Imabari Castle, but won't have enough time to explore any of the islands or the famous towel museum.

Ehime gets less rain than Kochi, which is actually quite good news at this point because my 'waterproof' shoes totally split and had to be thrown away. But that doesn't mean there's no rain at all. It can be quite wet between April and October, with June and July being peak typhoon season.

Fun fact: The Netflix drama 'Let's Get Divorced' is set in Ehime, following the trials and temptations of a political candidate as he campaigns in a local election. It's more fun than it sounds (honest!), but I mostly enjoyed it for the views of rice fields and country roads, and scenes shot in Matsuyama. It rains quite often in the drama, which I suspect is a true representation of the weather in March.

So, why am I here in Matsuyama, the city known as the Haiku Capital of Japan (more about that later, I promise)? Well, to be honest it's not because of my love of poetry. There's a castle! And by now you know I love Japanese castles, right?

Matsuyama Main Attractions Map

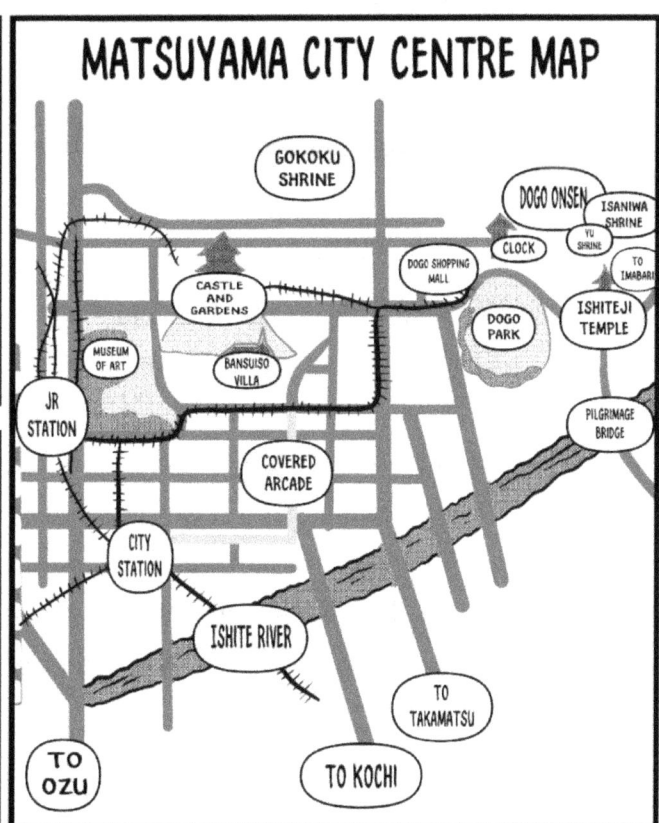

The other big attraction here is the Dogo Onsen Honkan, a public bathing building. It's the oldest and best known hot spring in Japan, partly because it was favoured by the Imperial Family over many years, and partly because of Studio Ghibli. If you watch the movie 'Spirited Away' by Hayao Miyazaki, the cartoon onsen was inspired by this real one. Cool eh? It's under reconstruction at the moment, which might thwart my plans to have a traditional onsen experience in a famous spa. But don't worry, I have a backup plan!

There's a famous novel set in Matsuyama (which I've not read) called 'Botchan', written by Natsume Soseki. You can buy tickets to ride on the 'Botchan Train' - a diesel replica of an old steam train which pulls old fashioned coaches from one side of Matsuyama to the other a few times a day. But an easier (and more comfortable) way to get around the city is by IYO Railway trams, some of which are modern while others are very old streetcars. There are five different tram lines (numbered 1,2,3,5 and 6) running around Matsuyama, and the fare is fixed regardless of how far you travel. It was 180 yen when I was there. Board the tram at the rear, and pay the exact fare as you leave through the door at the front. Use the convenient machines on the tram if you need change, preferably before the stop where you're getting off! There are also buses running around the city, but honestly a tram will probably get you anywhere you want to go.

Food!

Every prefecture in Shikoku has regional food specialities, and in Ehime this includes three types of noodle dishes. Nabeyaki udon is cooked in a sweet broth, Mitsuhamayaki okonomiyaki (cabbage pancake) is served with either soba or udon noodles, and Matsuyama ramen has a light soy sauce based slightly sweet broth. Ehime also has some fishy specialities, the best known of which are braised sea bream mixed into rice, and donburi featuring grilled eel on top of seasoned rice. Alan will be searching for that – it's a favourite of his.

If I need a sweet treat, I'll be on the lookout for Taruto (it's a cake, not an anime about a cat): a dessert resembling a swiss roll, made usually flavoured with red bean paste and yuzu. Botchan dango, another local speciality, consists of three rice dough balls on a stick, flavoured with red beans, egg, and green tea powder.

Over 40 varieties of citrus fruits are grown in Ehime, and different sorts of mikan are available throughout the year. I'm not a big fan of citrus fruits, but hopefully I'll get to try a small piece while I'm here.

Not Everything is Fish Food

Feeling a Little French

The coach dropped me off at the Okaido stop, just a couple of minutes walk from the Candeo Hotel where I'll be staying for the next four nights. This bright, modern hotel is conveniently located a few steps from a long shopping arcade, which is where Alan and I are currently enjoying a cheap Chinese style lunch. I was pleasantly surprised when the waitress asked me if I wanted no meat in my veg stir fry, and then yelled 'no meat in the vegetables!' towards the kitchen. I think I like Matsuyama already!

After popping back to the hotel to officially check in and take my luggage to the room, it's time to head partway up the nearby hillside to check out Bansuiso. This seemingly out-of-place French villa, which was built in the early 1990's by Count Hisamatsu Sadakoto, is the oldest reinforced concrete building in Ehime. It's quite pretty, with balconies, arches, and pointy bits on the roof. I enter via the porch flanked by Greek style pillars, and discover a large room with a display of hats from the 1900's, arranged on large round tables with white tablecloths. This room was originally the site of many parties for royalty and the social elite, including Emperor Showa while he was still a crown prince.

There's not really a lot to see inside the house, especially compared to stately homes in Europe and the UK, but it's a pleasant way to pass half an hour or so.

Bonus information: 'The Hound of the Baskervilles: Sherlock the Movie' (released in 2022) was filmed here. I've not seen it, so that's about all I can say about it!

How to be Stylish in a French Villa

Museum of Art

Next on today's relaxed agenda is the Ehime Museum of Art, which is in an impressive modern building with big windows and nice views. I can't claim to find the art collections exciting, and a member of staff has stalked us throughout our visit, making me feel a bit uncomfortable. I don't have any photos to remind me of what I've just seen, and I expect it will quickly fade away in my memory and just be classified as 'somewhere I went one afternoon'.

It's getting close to food-time, so I'm going to have a wander around a little park, then return to the shopping arcade near the hotel. I believe the biggest department store has a food court in the basement with an Okaido brewery stall and various fast food stands.

A Brew for Two

I know this hasn't been a very exciting day to read about, but sometimes I need the downtime which comes from changing cities partway through a trip. However, I do have something exciting to report before heading off to bed. I've tried the onsen! The hotel rules say 'tattoos must be covered' instead of 'tattoos strictly forbidden', so I thought I'd see if there was a way I could go in without causing too much upset. I asked the guy at reception how big the tattoo covers provided by the hotel are, persuaded him to give me 8 of the largest ones (another rule says a maximum of 2 per person, but....), randomly placed them over my ink, and went for a shower followed by a hot tub soaking session. I was pretty certain I would be alone – the hotel information page actually shows the how busy the onsen is in real time – and I was correct. When a couple of mothers with young children arrived I sneaked out while they were in the shower area, and I'm sure my ninja-like stealth ensured they never even knew I'd been there.

So, was it worth the effort? Honestly no, not for me. It was pleasant – you should try it if you get the chance – but it was very hot, smaller than I expected, with no flowing waterspouts or pretty decor, and I'll be scrubbing tattoo-cover glue off for days. The tub in the hotel bathroom is much longer and deeper than the blubbertub at the previous hotel, so I think I'll just soak alone without the need for huge tattoo-cover stickers.

Alan has just returned from his bathe. He says a little old lady was casually cleaning around the naked men in the onsen. All the other guys just totally ignored her and carried on as if she wasn't there so he did the same, although he found the experience a bit unusual to say the least.

Bashful Bathing

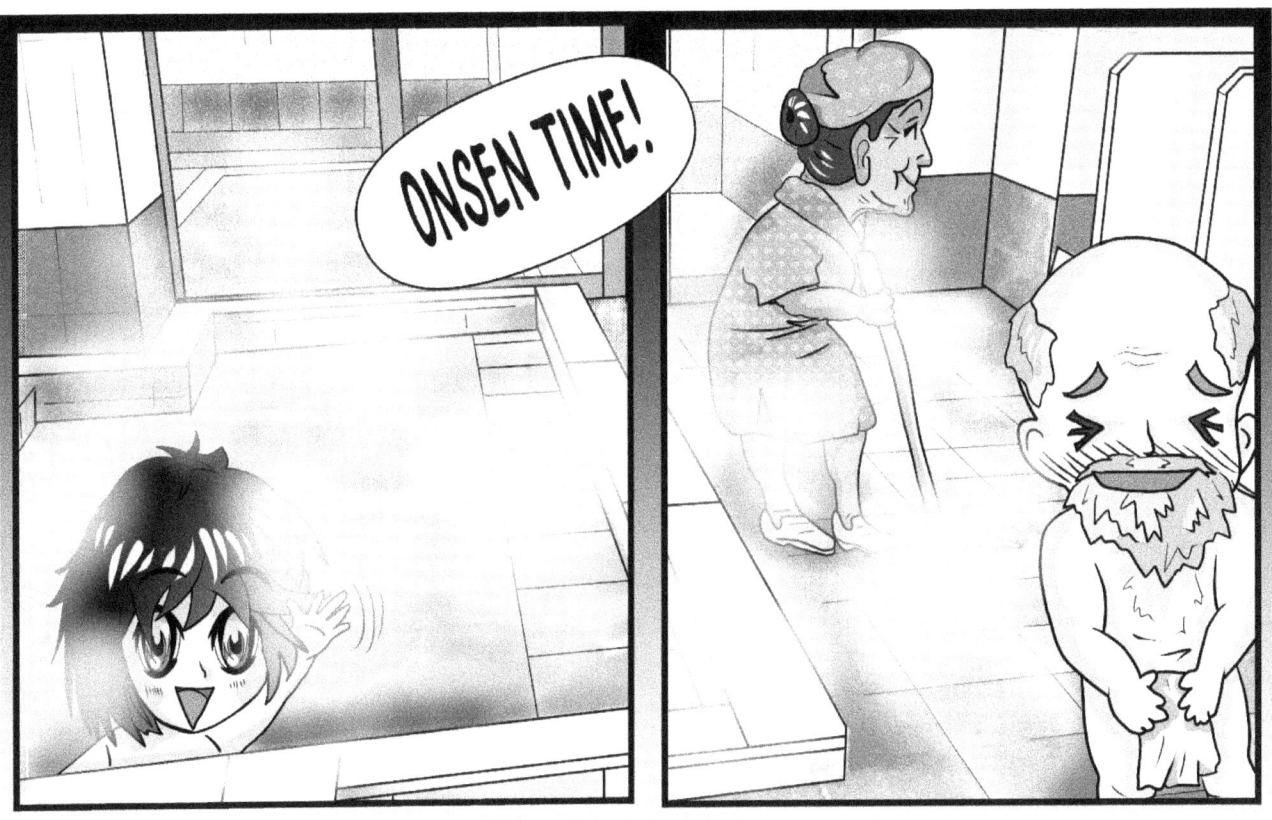

Matsuyama Castle day

Matsuyama ya
Aki yori takashi
Tenshukaku
Oh, Matsuyama, higher than autumn, the castle tower.
(Masaoka Shiki)

I've had a good night's sleep (waking way too early, of course) in a comfy king size bed and have headed down to the restaurant to grab some breakfast. Most people seated in the restaurant are dressed in the tunic and trousers provided by the hotel, and I have to admit that they fit small Asian bodies a lot better than big Caucasian ones. I'm much more comfortable in my travel pants and t-shirt. The Candeo buffet is very similar to the one in the Dormy inn, including both Japanese and continental items. I'm happy with my selection of vegetables, pickles, seaweed, fruit salad, tofu and rice. Alan has fish, fish, fish, fish and rice. And a couple of hot dogs.

Today I'm taking advantage of the pleasant weather and heading to the castle, which was the main reason for coming to Matsuyama. Construction started on this castle in 1602, at the top of Mount Katsuyama to provide good views of both the city below and the Seto Island Sea. It was under the command of the Matsudaira family until the end of the feudal period. It's considered to be one of Japan's 12 'original' castles, because it still has the original tenshu (keep / tower). I'm not convinced this is strictly speaking true – the current tower is three storeys high and was built to replace the five-story tenshu which was destroyed by lightning – but six watchtowers and some gates are definitely part of the original construction. Anyway, it's listed as one of Japan's top 100 castles, and I'm looking forward to checking it out.

It doesn't take long to walk to the entrance to the castle grounds, maybe 15 minutes. Alan and I arrive just ahead of a large tour group, and are lucky to get our tickets for the ropeway without having to wait in a long line. The tickets give us a choice of going up the mountain in a multi-person gondola, or in single person ski-lift chairs. We choose the latter because it sounds like much more fun. And it is! The chairlift seats don't have any safety bars or seatbelts, but there's a reassuring metal mesh between the chairs and the ground, so if anyone falls out they don't end up splattered over the lovely landscape.

Upon safely dismounting the chairlift (I've had lots of experience doing this sort of thing while wearing skis) I begin the climb up to the castle itself. I can see beautiful sakura blossoms, enormous stone walls, and a cruise ship docked in the distance. Uh oh. I think things are going to get very crowded soon!

I was right. I get into the castle just as a swarm of cruise ship sticker-wearing people start arriving at the ticket booth. I take off my shoes, put them in a locker, and head off into the keep. Alan has squished his feet into some tourist slippers, which resemble badly fitting flipflops, but my damaged foot really can't tolerate them so I'm going to slide around in my socks.

There's not really a lot to see inside the castle except historical information boards (in Japanese), some swords and armour displays, and some models of the castle and surrounding area, but the views through the peep holes and windows are lovely. From the top of the keep I can see the cherry blossom trees down in the grounds. They're in full bloom and look truly beautiful on this sunny day.

I've arrived back at the locker room ahead of Alan, and it's heaving with cruise ship tourists, some of whom are struggling with the 'take your shoes off' concept. I put mine back on and take a seat in the corner to wait for Alan. A lady plonks herself down next to me and starts talking. Apparently she's seen me on the cruise ship (!!!), and really likes my tattoos, and she's Australian, and there was no way she's climbing up that staircase, and she's got all kinds of allergies, and... She seems like a nice person, but it's a relief when the rest of her party climbs back down the stairs (they must have run through the castle – they've only been gone 5 minutes!), closely followed by Alan. I excuse myself and make my escape before someone decides to escort me back to the cruise ship where I apparently belong.

Footloose

I need a bit of refreshment after my close encounter of an Australian kind, and luckily the little gift shop has a cafe which serves zenzai and dango! Oh happy day.

After the delicious snack I walk down a winding path through the woodland to the castle gardens. The uneven stone steps and warning signs saying things like 'beware of nature animals' and 'look up for danger of trees falling on your head' make the walk a bit challenging, but it's fun.

It's only taken about 15 minutes to reach the Ninomaru Gardens at the base of Mount Katsuyama, constructed on the site where the castle offices and lord's residence used to be located. None of the original buildings remain, but the foundations have been turned into a rather unique water garden. There's also a traditional pond with koi swimming in the clear waters. And it's peaceful here – no cruise ship crowds, just a couple of young Japanese guys strolling around and a group of women having a picnic.

Marvellous Matsuyama Castle

Hanami

I'm getting hungry. 'Hanami' is on my to-do list, so I'm heading to some food trucks in the park to see if I can make it happen. I want to have a picnic under the sakura trees!

Celebrating flowers in full bloom is a really old tradition in Japan, which is thought to have begun around 710. Ume (plum blossoms) were the original flowers being admired, but by the Heian period (794-1185) sakura became more popular, to the point where the word 'flower' in a haiku is assumed to refer to sakura. During this era, Emperor Saga started having cherry blossom viewing parties underneath the trees in Kyoto's Imperial Court. The practice of 'hanami' quickly spread from royalty and samurais down to the common folk. More and more trees were planted throughout Japan, and picnicking under the blossoms became part of Japan's culture.

In modern times, lots of people can be seen sitting on large blue plastic sheets while munching on home-made or store-bought bento boxes, which I've always found a little strange. Why are the sheets bright blue and not cherry blossom pink? Japan is so focused on natural beauty and harmony, and the blue plastic clashes so badly with the gentle pink of the lovely flowers. It's an odd choice. I, however, don't have a sheet of any colour to sit on…

You can do hanami without a sheet, but you can't have a picnic without food! Owl cafe's food truck is really cute, decorated like the cat bus in Studio Ghibli's' 'My Neighbour Totoro' but I'm heading to a truck selling vegan falafels and pickled veg in pita bread (my lunch) and soy 'chicken' curry in pita (Alan's choice). It's time for a romantic break sitting on the grass in the sunshine under the pretty sakura trees. A couple of ladies sitting on a nearby bench are playing tunes on little mouth-harps, adding to the joyful spring festival atmosphere.

Trucking

Kururin Ferris Wheel

Next on the agenda is a walk to Iyotetsu Takashimaya. This luxury department store, located next to Matsuyama city station, is the largest of its kind in Ehime prefecture. It's *the* place to buy premium cosmetics, high-end fashion, electronic goods, books, and much more. But I'm not going there to shop. On the roof of this department store is the big Kururin ferris wheel, offering great views of the city. And – bonus – the ride is free if you show your passport!

A Wheelie Good Department Store

Well that was a fun day. I'm sitting here doing my end-of-day write-up while Alan soaks in the onsen. I chose to have a soak in our room's bathtub instead of covering myself with large sticky patches to use the onsen, and it was made extra nice by the strawberry bubble bath I picked up from the Body Shop in Iyotetsu. Dinner was a tasty tofu miso ramen ordered from a ticket machine at a cheap diner, followed by sugar-coated chestnut balls (not as exciting as I'd hoped) from a stall in the oh-so-incredibly-long covered shopping arcade.

I'm watching tv as I write, laughing out loud at a 'guess the kanji' game show. It's a game I play on a daily basis when wandering around Japan, with bonus rounds of 'read the hiragana' and 'try to decipher the katakana' (foreign words written in a Japanese script). When neither Alan nor I can work out what something says, I resort to using Google translate on my phone. Translation apps, while sometimes very useful, are often hilarious. For example, tonight's dinner's menu apparently included raw hydrogen, elderly care beer, human rotisary stick, and fried chicken knee. Actually the last one might have been a real thing...

Food for Thought

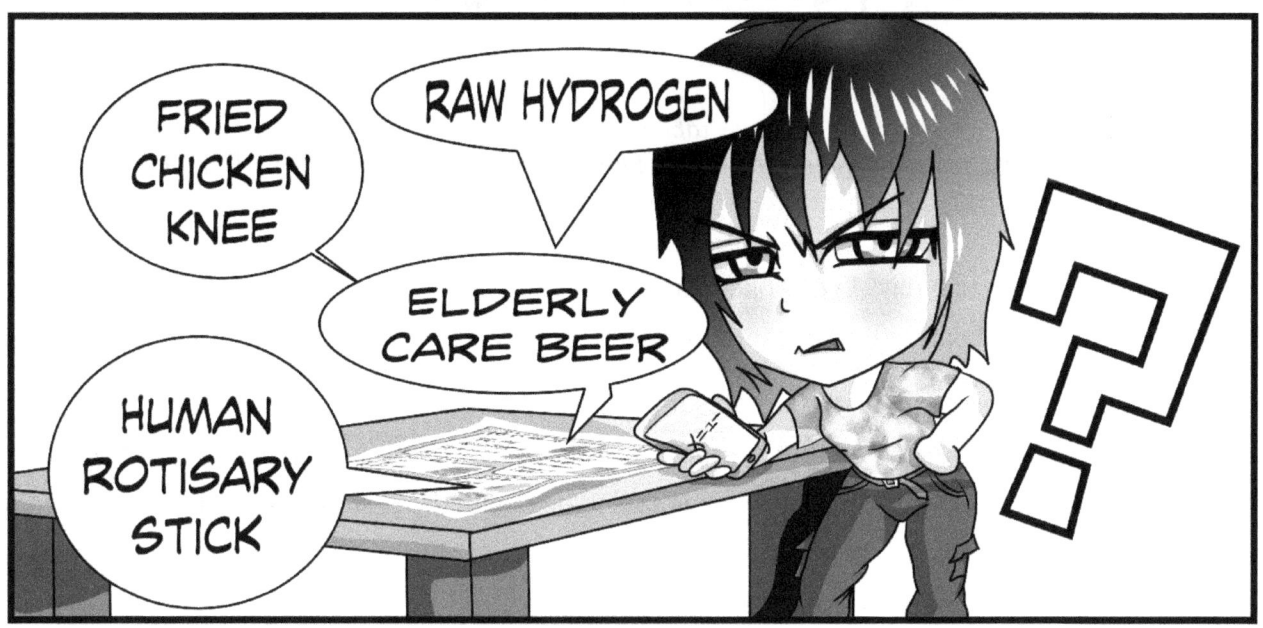

A Tale of Two Cities

hana no kage
utai ni nitaru
tabine kana
On a journey, resting beneath the cherry blossoms, I feel myself to be in a Noh play
(Matsuo Basho)

Today is dual town train trip day! I've applied surgical support tape to my foot in anticipation of lots of walking, taken a couple of painkillers, put suntan cream on my slightly burnt nose, and I'm raring to go.

"To where?" I hear you ask. The first point of call will be Ozu, an old castle town in the Nanyo region of Ehime. It was mostly built during the Edo period, and some of the historic alleyways and old houses still remain. A river flows through the middle, which is said to be one of the best places in Japan to see trained cormorants being used to catch fish in the summer. There's an old villa or two there which are apparently worth visiting. It also, of course, has a castle.

The second town of the day is Uchiko, located about 10km away from Ozu. It's another quaint little place with historic houses, and used to be an important site for the production of Japanese paper and tree wax. It's an 'Important Preservation District for Groups of Traditional Buildings', which sounds quite impressive! Unlike everywhere else I've visited so far on this trip, Uchiko has neither a castle (gasp!) nor one of the 88 pilgrimage temples. What is does have, however, is a very old theatre. More about that later...

It's going to take a bit of work to get to these two towns, and to start today's adventure I need to take a tram to the Matsuyama JR railway station, about 10 stops away. There are four trams which will be stopping in front of the hotel in the near future. Three will take me to where I want to go, and one will not.

Trams in Matsuyama (like everywhere in Japan) run on a very strict schedule, so when one arrives at the stop at the expected time Alan and I get on. 'This is going to Matsuyama Central' says the announcement. We turn to each other in confusion. Matsuyama Central is exactly NOT where we want to go. I look around and notice another tram sitting right behind the one we're on, and it's the one we actually need. We make a quick exit (through the entrance door, I'm ashamed to say) and leap onto the other tram just as the doors are closing.

That was a bit embarrassing, but now we're going in the right direction! I hope.

Ozu Castle

I'm now on a limited express train heading to Ozu, to see the castle! I'm not a history buff or into architecture, but I really like castles. This one was built in the Kamakura period (1185-1333) but over the years bits of it fell down, burnt down, got damaged in earthquakes, or just gave in to the tests of time. The great thing about Ozu castle is that it's been restored fairly recently, so I'll get to see what old Japanese castles looked like when they were new. It's been reconstructed using traditional techniques and materials, using old photos and paintings for reference, so the wooden interiors look like they did when it was first built.

It's taken about 40 minutes to get from Matsuyama to Iyo-Ozu station, passing through lots of really long tunnels through the mountains on the way. It's only a 20-minute walk from here to the castle, but I'm going to hop on the left loop local bus instead and save all the walking for later.

Simply Sakura

The bus trip was successful, dropping me near the base of the castle walls. It's the perfect day for photographing the beautiful sakura on the short walk from the bus stop up to the castle. When I was in Kochi the cherry blossoms were still mostly just buds, but here, today, under the blue skies of Ehime, with sunlight dappling the ground through the branches, they're just about perfect. Hurray!

By the time I get to the castle I'm thinking about lunch. The ladies in the garden cafe bring freshly grilled tofu and udon for me to eat under the cherry blossom trees, with petals gently wafting around on the breeze and landing on my food. Does life get any better than this?

Floral Lunch

And now it's time to head into the actual castle! The original tower was demolished in 1888, so the one I can see in front of me is completely new, and was finished in 2004. The four turrets, however, are all original (with a bit of recent repair work) and have been designated as 'Important Cultural Properties'.

Ozu castle lives up to all my expectations. There's only a few castles in Japan made entirely out of timber (many have been reconstructed using concrete) and this is one of them. The wood joists and floors positively gleam, the walls are the whitest of whites, and it feels quite opulent. The interior staircases are, as usual, very steep with some low beams, but at least they're level rather than being worn down with many years of use. There are exhibits on each floor of the keep telling the history of Ozu, some with miniature figures showing village life. There's also glass cabinets containing swords and armour which belonged to historical feudal lords.

Castle Life

The view of the town and river from the top of the four-story tenshu is, of course, fabulous.

I've seen a lot of Japanese castles, but this one definitely gets two thumbs up for being small but lovely. I've seen adverts for 'Castle Experiences' where you can actually arrive at the castle on horseback, dress in Samurai armour, and sleep in the castle itself or in one of the old houses in the street below with a view of the castle. There's no bathroom or kitchen in castle, but a luxury lounge and soaking tub has been built somewhere in the castle grounds. Breakfast is served in Garyu Sanso – a cliffside villa which is the next place on today's to-do list.

Oh Ozu!

Garyu Sanso and Bansenso

I've just had a lovely stroll (about 15 minutes) through old alleyways lined with ancient houses, heading from the castle to my next destination in Ozu. On one of the narrow streets I stopped in front of a sweet guy sitting on a step folding what looked like palm leaves to make grasshoppers. I said they were lovely and asked if he sold them. He smiled and led me to a little stall around the corner which was covered in grassy-hoppers. I chose one, paid the incredibly small amount he was asking, and was about to leave when he waved me to come back. He disappeared into his house and returned holding a bowl out of citrus fruit segments to share with Alan and me. It was the sweetest, softest, most fragrant citrus fruit (I think it was a mikan) I've ever eaten, and I fulfilled my wish to try a small piece of a local fruit!

I'll be giving the grasshopper to my eldest son when I get back home. I know he'll love to look at it on his desk while he's studying.

Grassy Grasshoppers

I've arrived at Garyu Sanso (garyu means resting dragon), which was built in the early 1900's on a beautiful spot near Mount Horai, overlooking the Hiji river (Hijigawa). It took 10 years to design this retirement dream home for a local merchant and over four years to actually build it. Three parts of this villa were given the designation of 'Important Cultural Property' in 2011.

The villa itself is really attractive, with a thick thatched roof and a walk-around veranda. It's very simple inside but aesthetically pleasing. On this lovely day the sliding doors are open, showing the beautiful view of the river. In one wall there's a circular window, which I'm told represents the moon. The two small teahouses are also nice, but the best one is at the end of the garden, resting on stilts and overlooking the river down below. There's only a couple of other people here, and it's really tranquil.

I wish I could linger, but now... on to Bansenso!

This attractive residence, about a five-minute amble from the Garyu Sanso, sits at the top of a hill and also overlooks the river. It was built in the 1920's by two brothers who made their fortunes running a trading company in the Philippines and wanted a holiday home back in Japan. They used timber imported from Asia to build a three-story house which has a lot of traditional Japanese features like tatami mats and sliding screens. There's also some foreign design influences and ideas, including a private area for women to prepare themselves to greet guests after bathing. I think something got lost in translation here, because I'm not sure if it was the women or the guests who were doing the bathing, or if women usually just climbed out of the tub to greet guests while wet? Anyway, there are screens here which are 'considerate to women', and that's always a good thing. Another unique feature of this home is the fresh water system flowing from a well inside a cave (a guide let me look inside) into a water tank in the kitchen. It's kinda cool.

I'm typing notes on my phone while sitting on the home's balcony, which was very unusual feature for a Japanese home in the 20's (Taisho era). It's got a great view, and a gentle breeze is blowing. I wish I could stay longer, but I'm going say a quick goodbye to a lion statue in the garden and wander down the hill. Hopefully I'll arrive at a stop for the loop bus in about five minutes, which will take me back to the train station. And then... on to Uchiko!

Beautiful Buildings of Ozu

Uchiko

I had a drama-free trip back to the JR station (It was the same bus and driver as on the way to the castle) to catch the limited express train to Uchiko. And now it's time for some actual drama! My main reason for coming here is to see an ancient kabuki theatre with a rotating stage, hand-powered pop-up platforms, and original wooden seating. It was built in 1916 to celebrate Taisho becoming Emperor and, despite being refurbished in 1985, looks the same now as it did then. There are 20 traditional kabuki theatres remaining in Japan, but this one is one of only a few which still hold performances.

It's taken about 10 minutes to walk here along deserted streets from the JR station, and it's not long until the theatre closes for the day so I'm not pausing to look at the (closed) cultural museums and houses along the way. It would be sad to come all this way and not actually be allowed into the theatre!

The outside of the building looks impressive, with paintings of Kabuki plays under a sloping roof and brightly coloured flags blowing in the breeze in front of dark wooden beams and white walls. There's still 30 minutes until closing time, so I buy a ticket, take my shoes off, and head inside.

The main hall contains a large stage of gleaming wood, in front of which are rows of boxes on the floor for the audience to sit in to watch performances. I've sat in something similar to watch a sumo basho in Fukuoka, and I would strongly suggest not trying to fit more than two people into a box which officially seats four.

There are costumes for visitors to wear, so Alan treats me to a short performance on the stage while wearing a stylish jacket. It was entertaining, but I don't think he should quit his job to join the theatre.

One of the nice things about this building is that visitors can go underneath the stage to see the trap doors, dark passageways and hand-cranked mechanisms which revolve the centre of the stage. It's all very cool, and worthy of a short visit on the way back from Ozu to Matsuyama.

There are other historical properties in Uchiko, but nothing is open this late in the afternoon. If you go, perhaps you could check out the Takahashi merchant's residence or the Museum of Commercial and Domestic Life. That one is probably a lot more fun than it sounds. I walked past it on the way from the train station and it has life-size waxwork people standing in a replica of a pharmacy in the large window.

Acting Cool

It's getting late, and I'm getting hungry. Again. I wander around the old streets for a while, and Alan tries (and fails) to find an open restaurant on Google Maps. We eventually find an old izakaya close to station and the sign outside says it's open. Huge sigh of relief! However, when I step inside there are no lights on. The head of a tiny, wrinkled old lady pops up from behind the counter. "I'm very sorry to interrupt, but are you open?" "I am now, please come in," she says as she turns on the lights. It looks like she'd just been sitting in the kitchen in the dark, and had definitely not been expecting customers. I balance myself on a bar stool made out of a tree trunks, which was designed for bottoms smaller than mine, and accept a proffered menu. I'm quite tired, so I take the lazy way out and ask Google to translate it for me. I think Google is also tired because it's doing a total half-assed job of it. I give up when it says there is 'rotten salad', but then spot a kanji I recognise. "Do you have tofu?" I ask. "Yes! I'll bring you tofu!"

The tofu is buried under mounds of katsuobushi (shaved dried fish), but it's nicely chilled and fresh. I'm very happy. Okonomiyaki (cabbage pancakes) is decipherable at the bottom of the menu, so I've ordered a regular one and Alan has asked for one with soba noodles. Okonomiyaki can contain just about anything (the approximate translation is 'as you like it'), but by the time I've requested no mayonnaise I've run out of enthusiasm for further requests and decide to just go with the flow. I can quietly dig out anything like squid or octopus should the need arise.

And now, full of pancake, tofu and beer, I'm going to catch a train back to Matsuyama and have a long relaxing soak in my strawberry scented private bathtub while Alan heads off to the onsen. It's been another lovely day.

Is Anyone There?

Imabari Birthday Castle!

Haru no umi
Hinemosu notary
Notary kana
The spring sea all day rising and subsiding
(Yosa Buson)

This morning, after another yummy breakfast, I caught the 8:20am tram to the JR station, and from here I'll take the limited express train to Imabari. Alan is currently in the shinkansen reservation office booking seats on a train to Marugame on Tuesday. Reserved seats cost quite a bit more than unreserved, but it's going to be quite a long trip and we don't want to risk having to stand up for all or part of the way.

Today, for a special birthday treat, I'm going to see a castle. Yes, another castle, but not just any castle – this is one of only three mizujiro (castles next to the sea) in Japan! As a bonus I'll also get to see another of the 88 pilgrimage temples, and hopefully get another lovely piece of calligraphy in my book.

Nankobo

Temple 55, known as Nankobo, is about a five-minute walk from the train station. Fun fact: it's the only one of the temples on the Shikoku pilgrimage which has 'bo' in its name, meaning 'priest lodging'. It was originally built closer to the sea but was moved to its current location so the rituals wouldn't be influenced by waves and winds. It burned down, along with a lot of Ehime, in a big fire in the 1500's. The temple was rebuilt but sustained major damage during World War II. The main hall was rebuilt in 1981.

It's 55 Time!

There's a lovely cherry blossom tree next to the main gateway (which was rebuilt in 1998) where four Niomon stand guard. The central courtyard appears to be a parking lot surrounded by small shrines. I can see lots of lovely wood carvings, stone buddhas wearing red bibs, a statue of a pilgrim who appears to be wearing a medical face mask, and all the usual trimmings found in a Buddhist temple. This 'Temple of Southern Light' is a huge sprawling complex, but I'm going to get my Henro book signed and wander off. Temples are ok, but there's a castle to see!

A Mizujiro Castle

It was a five-minute walk from the temple to the bus stop, followed by a scenic ride along the coastline to the castle.

The beautiful white buildings are surrounded by a wide, square moat, filled with seawater. It's tidal, and I can see a wet line around the stone walls from earlier in the day when the water level was higher. Obviously the tide never completely empties the moat – that would have made it hilariously easy for feuding lords to attack the castle on low-tide day! There are fish in the moat, and a sign instructs people not to remove them.

A Castle without a Hill

There's a number of buildings in the castle grounds, so I buy tickets to enter all of them then race to the top of the main keep to stay ahead of a large group of tourists. It's easier to admire a beautiful view without lots of other people's heads in the way. And what a view it is! The sea is shining under the bright blue skies, and down in the courtyard I can see a big shrine and other castle buildings. A big statue of Todo Takatora on a horse is clearly visible from up here. He fought in wars for various feudal lords, but is best known for designing and building castles, including this one in Imabari.

Todo San!

The construction of this castle began in 1602 and finished in 1604. It had a lot of innovative features including an extra-wide moat to reduce the damage to the castle walls by soldiers with guns, and sluice gates to control the water level. I suspect the original tenshu was impressive, because shortly after completion it was taken down and rebuilt in Kyoto.

Imabari castle was abandoned after the Meiji restoration and many of the buildings fell down. A watch tower in one of the corners survived and was used as an armoury until the gunpowder stored within blew up and demolished it in 1871. The current tenshu was built in 1980 but concrete was used instead of the traditional wooden structure, which I guess was cheaper, easier, and less likely to burn to the ground. The current castle gate, guard houses and watchtowers were rebuilt based on old photographs in the late 1900's and early 2000's.

I make my descent back down, pausing to look at display cases of armour and swords, and pass the group of tourists who had made it as a far as the 3rd floor but were heading back down because they didn't see the point of going all the way to the top. Oh well, their loss.

I'd spotted a ramen place located across the road from the castle from my viewpoint at the top of the tenshu, and it didn't take much effort to persuade Alan to come here for lunch. It's yet another mom and pop place run by a wizened old lady, with locals sitting at tables reading the newspaper or watching the TV while slurping noodles. She looked a bit worried as she handed us the Japanese menu (no pictures), but laughed when Alan showed her Google Translate on his phone. We were given a large jug of what looked like green swamp water but tasted of tea, and ordered lunch. My stir fried vegetables lunch, unsurprisingly, contains chunks of meat. Alan's soggy shrimp tempura floating in soup with udon is, apparently, very delicious. And judging from the drops of soup being flicked onto his t-shirt by the fat noodles, we'll be doing laundry again fairly soon.

Lunch break is over, so I'm heading back to the castle! There's a small natural history museum with stuffed creatures and fossils to check out, the Shinto shrine, and a couple of other buildings. The sun is still shining and it's the perfect day for wandering around this pretty place.

Fukiage-jinja Shinto shrine was built within the old walls of Imabari castle after it was abandoned during the Meiji restoration period. It's a Shinto shrine (not an 88 temple pilgrimage place), with a long row of small bright red torii gates and kitsune (fox) statues. These statues usually come in pairs, one with an open mouth and the other with it closed. Their tails often point into the air and a paw rests on a symbolic item. There's additional stone animals dotted around, one of which looks like a happy lion-dog creature.

I don't really have a lot more to say about this shrine, to be honest. The main hall has white walls, red beams and pillars, and a traditional roof, and somehow I seem to be following all the 'go this way' arrows in the wrong direction. It's my birthday, so perhaps my age is catching up with me...

Shinto Shrine Time

I'm back at Matsuyama JR station now, relaxing in a comfy chair in an English tea shop and enjoying treats from the 'happy cookies' menu. It really feels like I'm taking a mini-break in London, except that I can see Japan through the large windows. I can get free refills for my tea, and Alan looks like he's enjoying the downtime, so I might be here for a while.

Birthday Cookies

Teatime is over (there were too many cookies on my plate, so I've stashed the extras in my bag for snack-emergencies) and I'm about to implement a cunning plan. One of Matsuyama's main attractions is the Dogo Onsen Honkan, but it's currently under renovations, thwarting my plans to book a private bath there. There is, however, a new Annex with special private rooms which can be booked by phone a few days in advance. And this is where my cunning plan comes into play...

In the railway station, not far from the English tearoom, is a tourist information office, with a handy lady who speaks fluent English and Japanese. My Japanese is not up to the task of making specific reservations by phone, so I recruit her for the job. She's on the phone for a long time, asking me questions from every now and again, and engaging in long discussions with the person on the other end of the line. She finally turns to me. "Monday, 3pm, 2nd floor private bath and relaxation room, 90 minutes?" Yes!!! Ok, it's booked. There's no soap or shampoo allowed in this special bath, so Alan and I will have to shower before we go, or use the public shower room in the old part of the onsen. Then we present ourselves at the front door, and go in!

But back to today's adventures! I've hopped on a tram and am back in the shopping district near the castle, not far from the hotel. The other day I spotted a little shop selling noren (I know I already bought a Rilakkuma divided curtain in Kochi, but I 'need' more...) and I promised myself I'd spend some of my birthday money there. There's a few I like, and they're not expensive, and they'll probably fit into my suitcase, so Alan and the storekeeper are trying to work out how to pay on the store's antique credit card machine using a foreign card. It looks like the trick is to press the red (or is the green?) button to select the currency. Credit cards *can* be used in Japan, but cash is still king.

For my birthday dinner we've walked a couple of minutes to Coco Curry, where I know I can get a veg curry and a beer without much effort, but it turns out I've forgotten how difficult it can be for first-timers. The ladies at the next table are really struggling and the waitress is starting to look distressed, especially when one of the customers stands up and declares she's leaving. I ask if I can help. She's frustrated that she can't make herself understood. English isn't her first language, and she speaks no Japanese, so I hand her my phone with Google Translate open and tell her to type what she wants. A very spicy curry with shrimp. The waitress reads the Japanese translation, and everyone is happy again.

My birthday cake, eaten back at the hotel, is a tiny slice of pre-packaged naruto which I bought from the train station gift shop. Alan and I agree that we've had more exciting cakes.

Curtains, Curry and Cake

Moving On, but Not Far

to no kuchi ni
yado fuda nanore
hototogisu
on the inn's doorway a name card to announce yourself cuckoo
(Matsuo Basho)

We're up bright and early as usual, checked out of the Candeo Hotel, and at the ticket office for the castle ropeway when it opens at 8:30. We enjoyed our ride so much the other day that we've decided to do it again before we relocate to the Dogo Onsen area of the city for two nights. This time we're going to ride it both up and down, instead of walking down to see the gardens. Don't worry – we're not going to take our suitcases on the little chair lift with us, we've left them at the hotel. There's actually signs at the chair lift saying suitcases are not allowed, so some people must have attempted it in the past.

We're back at the base of the hill with a bit of time to spare before we need to retrieve our bags and catch a tram, so we're browsing in the tourist shops as we wander back. There's a large store selling products made in Imabari at the towel museum (it was too far from the castle to sensibly get to without a car), but I'm not going to buy anything here. Our bags are already full to capacity with towels Alan bought for his kenjutsu (japanese sword fighting) buddies at the train station yesterday, along a few noren, a couple of cd's, and a few small cute things. I don't think it's possible to visit Matsuyama without buying a kawaii squishy mikan animal. It looks like an orange hamster, and it's really cute. I should try to not buy anything else or I'll need another trip to a post office.

Fitting In

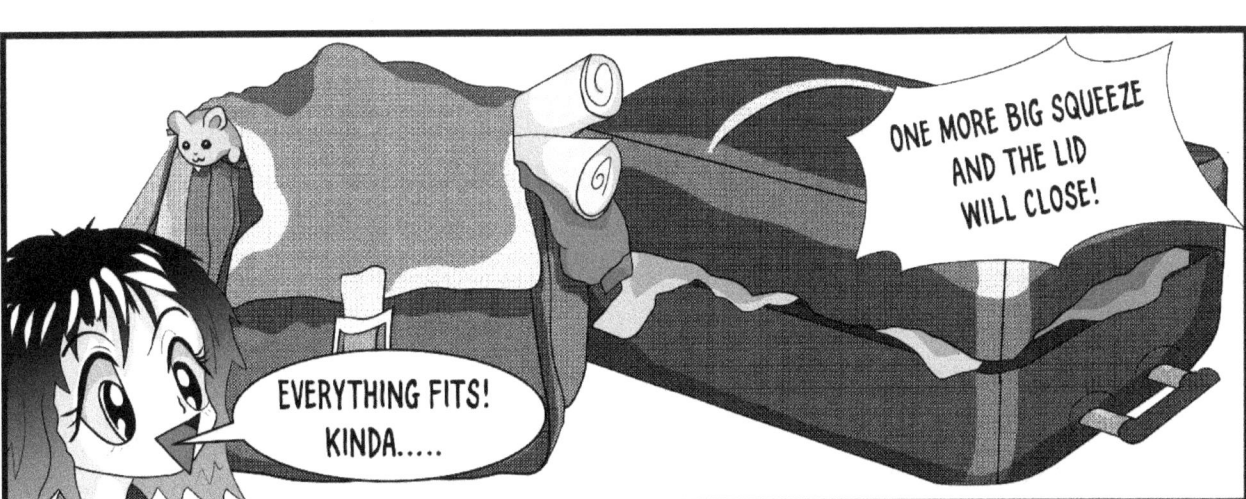

The tram ride to the Dogo Onsen area took about 10 minutes, and then there was an eight-minute walk up a quite steep hill to our home for the next two nights. This is my birthday-treat ryokan relaxation time, rejuvenating both of us for the final part of our trip. So far it's been day after day of go-go-go, usually starting at 6:30 in the morning and ending with us exhausted and asleep by 10:30 at night. The luggage is now safely stowed in the hotel's storage room, and I'm off to do some exploring.

The Dogo Onsen suburb of Matsuyama is a lot more touristy than the area around the castle. There's a studio Ghibli store (I might have to return and buy a couple of cute things) and a bench outside another store has Rilakkuma and friends sitting on it. At the bottom of the hill is Dogo Park, with a little river and lots of lovely cherry blossom trees. I think the park is on the ruins of Yuzuki Castle, but don't quote me on that. It's crowded with groups of people, sitting on blue plastic sheets and picnicking on food bought from the food stalls and trucks, although there's some people opening bento boxes filled with food brought from home. Petals are blowing around in a breeze, so pretty that they're worthy of a poem or two.

Shiki Museum

Talking of poems, in the introduction to Matsuyama I mentioned that it's known as the Haiku Capital. 'What's a haiku?' I hear you ask. Well, it's three-line poetry with five syllables in the first and third line and seven in the second line. In the 13th century the 'hokku' was the first part of much, much longer poems, but over time these lines started being written as poems in their own right. In 1666 a samurai called Matsuo Basho (born in Matsuyama) hung up his sword, picked up his pen, and transformed himself from a soldier into a poet. He wrote hokku based on his travels around Japan, and is largely responsible for the popularity of the three-line style of poetry.

It wasn't, however, until the 1800's that hokku became haiku, refined and renamed by another of Matsuyama's famous poets – Masaoka Shiki. There's a museum in the park dedicated to his life and works, and that's where I'm heading now.

Alan assures me it's a small museum which won't take long, knowing my attention span can be quite short in such places. If you're interested, you can rent an English audio guide, but here's the condensed version of what it says: Born in 1867 in Ehime (called Iyo back then), Shiki played baseball as a teenager, got TB, started studying haiku at the age of 18, wrote nearly 20,000 stanzas, became one of the most famous poets in Japan, was pivotal in developing haiku as a modern art form, and died in 1902 at the age of 34 after a lifetime of coughing up blood. He gave himself the pen name Shiki (little cuckoo) because he'd heard that cuckoos sing so hard that they vomit blood. (I really don't think they do that!) He believed that poetry should be written in contemporary language, and should reflect the realities of life. If you've been paying attention you'll have already spotted some of his haiku in this book, but here's a bonus one:

Poetic Sakura

Botchan Clock

And now, tick tock, it's time to see a clock! I'm standing in a crowd of people in front of a big tourist attraction – the Botchan clock – waiting for it to do something other than just tell the time. It was constructed in 1994, so it's a fairly recent addition to this old part of town, in celebration of Dogo Onsen Honkan's 100th anniversary.

As the big hand hits 6 (the performance happens every 30 minutes during the day), it lights up and the clock tower triples in height to the sound of taiko drumming. Doors open on the front, back and sides and characters from the Botchan novel tell their stories. It's all in Japanese but it's fun to watch, especially the guys in a hot tub (not real ones!) in the clock base. The grand finale is when a lady at the top of the clocktower welcomes us all to the town and then the clock folds back in on itself and shrinks to its original size.

I consider dipping my feet in the spring water footbath next to the clock now that the excitement is over, but I decided against it for a couple of reasons. 1: I don't have a towel. 2: it's currently being used by a group of obviously unwell tourists who pull down their masks, sneeze onto their hands, then pull their masks back up. Argh! I'm wearing a mask, but when one sneezes in my direction I idly wondered what the incubation period is for the virus they're sharing so freely. (Spoiler alert – it's 3 days.)

I have some time to fill before checking in at the hotel, so I wander up the hill to the Dogo Giyaman Glass Museum. The shallow tiled pool outside the museum is very pretty, but the museum itself isn't very big. It's basically a long room with glass cabinets containing small things also made out of glass. There's about 300 pieces, some of which date back to the Edo period, but it's probably not worth going unless you really love old glass vases and bowls, or if you have nothing better to do with your time, which I don't.

Tick Tock Magic Clock

Back at the hotel, we show our passports, sign a form, and are welcomed to Dogo Onsen Yachiyo. The room is ready, and the luggage has already been taken up for us.

After a bit of bowing by the reception staff we're escorted to the sixth floor, stopping on the way to choose what colour and pattern of yukata (lightweight kimono-like robe) we would like to wear while here. It's the first time ever that I've found a woman's pretty pattern yukata in my size in a Japanese hotel or ryokan. I've mentioned before that I'm quite tall, which is ok in Canada but can sometimes be a bit of an issue in Asia. Here in the Yachiyo I have to select from the tallest category, but for once I don't have to dress like a guy!

The room is beautiful, exactly as it appears on the hotel website. Bamboo blinds, futon beds on a raised platform, modern sleek furniture, a European style dining table, and a private outdoor onsen. I instantly feel more relaxed than I have for days.

One of the lovely things about this ryokan (in addition to the service, the beautiful room, the private outdoor bath, and the gender-appropriate yukata) is that tattoos are allowed into the public bath. So that's where I'm heading as soon as I've finished a lovely sakura sweet and small cup of tea served in our room as a welcome gift.

The bath was lovely. I chose the outdoor one (it's screened from prying eyes, so don't imagine it's just sitting out in a wide open space!) which was beautifully hot and relaxing. I was alone, but it was nice to know that if someone else entered my inked skin wouldn't be a problem. Now I just have to stay awake until dinner.

Totally Chillaxing

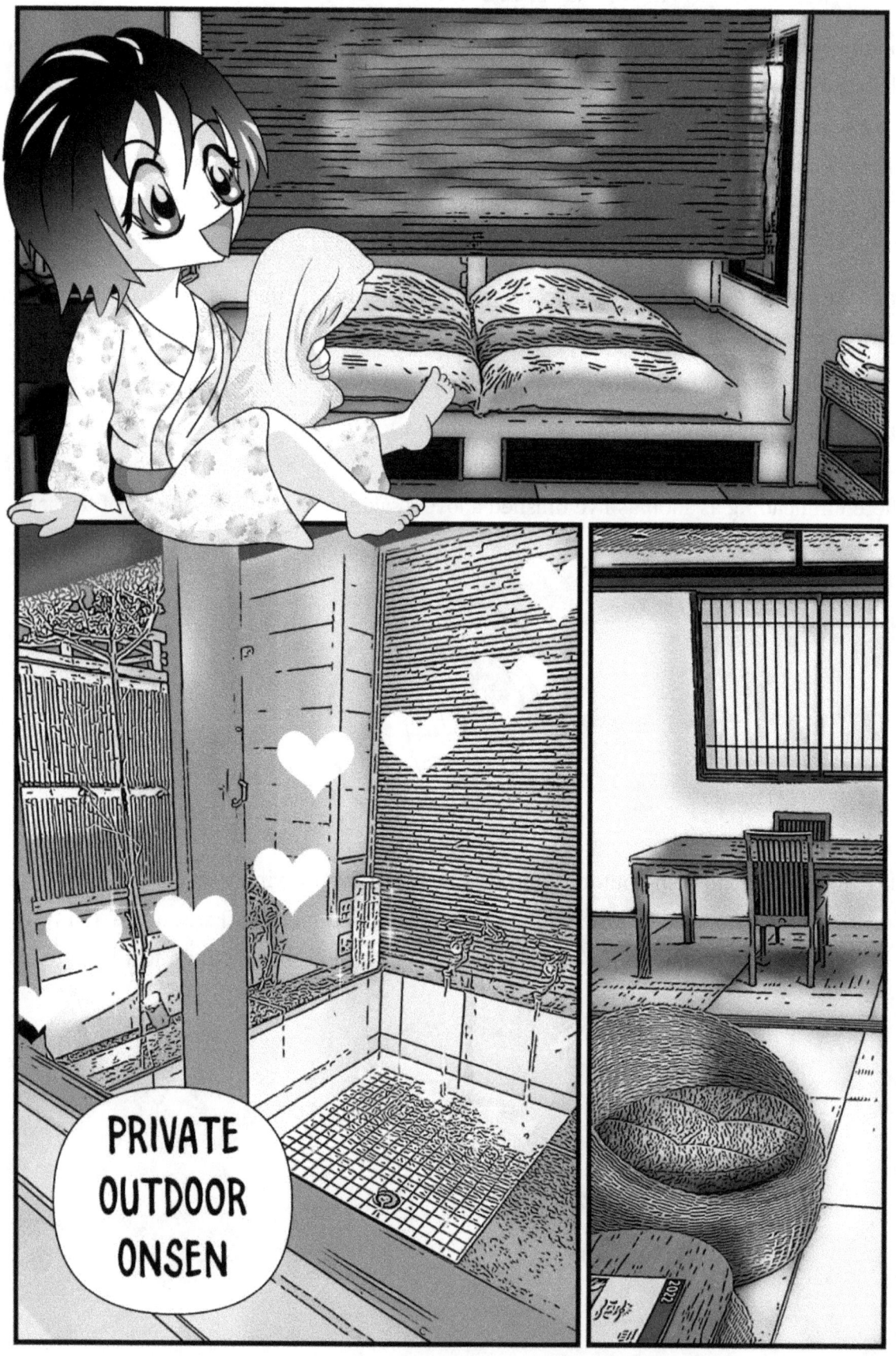

PRIVATE OUTDOOR ONSEN

Dinner, served in our room one course at a time, was spectacular. If I was an Instagrammer this meal would have been turned into photos and posted on social media immediately, with exclamations like #FoodPorn and #FabFood.

This is one of those occasions where I might overshare about a meal, but it has nothing to do with the bottle of sake I added to the hotel bill. Whish was, I might add, weally velly good sake!

The appetizer consisted of numerous tiny bowls containing morsels of locally grown seasonal vegetables and seafood from the Seto Inland Sea, purchased this morning. There was tofu paste with bracken, prawns with rape blossom, bamboo shoots with miso sweet potato, grilled sea bream, grilled chicken with slated malt, and cherry blossom mochi! No, my Japanese translation skills haven't suddenly improved dramatically – the menu was presented in both Japanese and English.

You might have already deduced this, but I'm not someone who eats 'everything', and Alan isn't a huge fan of fruit or salad, and I was a bit worried that hostess would remain in the room while we dined. Luckily, after she presented each course she left to prepare the next one, allowing Alan and I to peacefully swap things from one plate to another without causing offense.

Everything was amazing, beautifully presented on simple tableware which complemented the appearance of the food. Sashimi, simmered eggplant with pork, vinegared sardine with lemon, grilled rice ball in a clear soup, pickles, sea bream soup, and a traditional Ehime pork stew under a puff pastry crust. There was a surprise dish not shown on the menu, which at first I thought was deep fried chicken but turned out to be battered morsels of fugu (blowfish). As you're probably aware, fugu can only be prepared by chefs with special training and a license because, improperly prepared, it can be toxic. And how was it? Alan loved it...

The final course was only thing which contained something neither of us would eat – a small blob of cream which was perched on top of some fresh fruit. Our hostess laughed. She doesn't eat dairy either.

I'm finishing up the incredible dining experience with some hot green tea. I think when Alan and I have sobered up a bit we'll try our private onsen. Maybe we'll be able to see some stars through the bamboo privacy wall.

(We couldn't.)

Dining in Style

Ishiteji and Onsen Day

ara nantomo na ya
kinō wa sugite
fukuto-jiru
oh, nothing's happened to me! yesterday has passed – fugu soup
(Matsuo Basho)

Foreshadowing Fugu

Will there be more fugu in this chapter? Maybe. You'll just have to wait and see…

I woke later than usual, having slept peacefully on the comfortable thick soft futon. Breakfast was served in the room, which was a really nice change from lurching off to a breakfast buffet with lots of other people. It wasn't all to my taste, but that was ok. My loss was Alan's gain.

Even though we're staying here another night, I'm currently packing my suitcase and non-essential items ready for dropping them off at reception this afternoon before 4pm. I want to do a daytrip to Marugame on the way to our next hotel in Takamatsu, and it's easier to send my luggage on ahead than leave it in a train station locker while I go exploring. The bags will be picked up by a courier from Japan's efficient Takkyubin service and will (hopefully!) be waiting for me in Takamatsu tomorrow evening. Just a little tip: Takkyubin don't currently pick up from, or deliver to, an Airbnb, but you can ship to and from some convenience stores. I'll be sending my iPad on ahead, so today's and tomorrow's notes will be typed on my phone. The screen is very small, so wish me luck!

Ishiteji

Today is beautifully sunny, the perfect weather for visiting Matsuyama's best known temple. It was a five-minute walk from the ryokan to the bus stop followed by a short bus ride, and now I'm at Temple 55 – Ishiteji! According to folklore, 'stone hand temple' was given its name after a rich man died while holding a stone in his hand and was reborn as a baby while still holding the stone. It sounds a bit unlikely to me, but perhaps the expanded version will make it more believable? A wealthy landlord was mean to a beggar, and as a result his eight sons died. He went to find Kukai (Kobo Daishi) to ask for forgiveness and still hadn't found him after four years of walking around Shikoku in a clockwise direction. So he tried walking anticlockwise, and when he collapsed with exhaustion Kukai appeared and forgave him. He wrote something on a stone which he placed in the dying man's hand. Sometime later a baby was born holding the same stone, and when the child grew up he paid for the Annyo temple to be restored and renamed it Ishiteji. I'm not sure any of that makes it more believable, but it does explain why every four years it's considered lucky to do the 88 temple pilgrimage in reverse order, going anticlockwise around Shikoku.

It looks like an interesting place, even though I've not yet made it past the large dragon statue towering over me at the entrance. It's all the more impressive because there's a carving of a goddess standing on the dragon's head. Other statues are scattered around the area, including some stone Jizo wearing red bibs and one of Kobo Daishi. This temple is already my favourite. It's got a really cool vibe to it. I've heard it described as 'zany', and I can see why.

I walk along the short covered shopping street (most of the stalls still have their shutters down this early in the day) to the Niomon gate. It's a designated national treasure, but to my untrained eye it looks very similar to many similar gates I've encountered on my travels. What makes it stand out for me, though, are the huge (bigger than me) straw sandals propped up on either side of the gateway. According to mythology, if you touch them your leg ailments will be cured. I'm not sure this applies to feet, so I don't bother rubbing a giant sandal.

On the other side of the Niomon there's a courtyard with a firepit in the middle, scenting the air with incense, and colourful flags adorn little shrines. There's a lovely red pagoda rising up towards the sky, and a lot of strange carved wooden figures seem to have congregated outside the small shrines to admire it. I read somewhere that they resembled badly carved gnomes, and I can understand what the author meant! There's also lots of small, considerably less scary looking statues dotted around the walls and steps, including children's toys, action figures, and some really cute little plastic Buddhas surrounded by smooth rocks and pebbles. One of the shrines here (I'm not sure which one) has the 'Deity of Maternal Value' hidden inside. Women can take a pebble from the temple and then return with two stones if they give birth safely.

Lady on a Dragon's Head, and More!

The shrine directly in front of the pagoda allegedly contains a secret statue of Kobo Daishi. It's so secret that even the priests haven't seen it. But I'm sure it's really in there... right?

All this is lots of fun and very interesting, but my real reason for coming here is to check out a secret tunnel leading to a hidden inner temple. I don't see the tunnel at first – it's a secret, so that doesn't surprise me too much – until I accidentally stumble upon it hidden behind an unassuming-looking bamboo screen. The actual tunnel entrance has a statue of Kobo Daishi standing above it, with two bright red metal gates flanking a low narrow opening into the hillside. It looks kinda dark in there, but I place an offering (think of it as a voluntary entrance fee) in a box and venture inside.

It was indeed quite dark!!! I'm walking slowly and carefully through the dimly lit passage, trying very hard not to dislodge any of the Jizo statues standing on pedestals along the way. They're placed sort-of in the middle of the pathway but not in a straight line, and parts of the tunnel are really quite dark, so it's a bit of an adventure! Some of the pedestals are empty, possibly as the result of a collision with a pilgrim's backpack. About halfway along the tunnel is a bit wider and higher, and there's a life-size stone figure wearing a red bib. It's a bit (but only a bit) brighter here thanks to a small sting of lights hanging from the ceiling. And then it's back into darkness and little Jizos on plinths...

It's taken me almost five minutes to reach the other end, but I've emerged into daylight, popping out of the hillside through a hole hidden from sight behind a strange stone and concrete altar. I'd expected to find myself in a temple courtyard, but I'm actually on a peaceful country road. I can see a large Kobo Daishi statue on a far away hilltop, but just across the tarmac from me there's an impressive metal gateway with a large stone guy wearing a big hat perched on top of it. He looks a bit like a cowboy but I'm sure he's not. I'm assuming that's the way to the 'inner temple', so I'm heading off down the overgrown path.

And... Gosh! I've found the 'inner temple', or maybe it's something else altogether given that it's not actually in the temple complex? It's a large gold dome-shaped building with two fierce-looking gold lions guarding the door. There's a sign (written in many languages) hanging on the door saying 'Staff Only'.

The gravel courtyard is surrounded by countless weird wooden figures, some of which look happy and others look sad or angry. I don't know what they are, but maybe daemons, gnomes and gods? Sitting off to the right is a bigger-than-lifesize stone statue of a very thin guy (all his ribs are beautifully carved) sitting cross legged on a platform. I believe this is Buddha before he became enlightened, but it might be Ippen, founder of one of the sects of Buddhism. Anyway, the whole place is a bit odd.

I return to the road, sneak behind the altar and re-enter the dark tunnel. There's a second tunnel branching off the main one near the exit, leading to a spooky dark cave with religious statues standing behind bars in an eerie light. Maybe this is actually the 'inner temple'? I'm not a fan of this place, so I'm hoping the tunnel on my right will lead me back into the sunlight in the main temple complex.

Darkness, and Light (and a Golden Dome!)

I've popped out of the hillside behind one of the small shrines. What a strange place Ishiteji is! I think if you're going to visit one, and only one, of the 88 pilgrimage temples you should chose this one! I can't imagine any of the others being more entertaining.

There's still more to see here, and my attention has been drawn to one of the large egg-shaped marble objects sitting on stone plinths. This particular one has been placed in front of a large wooden statue (a bodhisattva perhaps?), and I watch as a lady climbs through a round polished stone donut (it's like a miniature stargate, but without an intergalactic portal) and bows to the deity on the other side. Alan takes off his hat and decides to also show some respect to the shiny egg and wooden figure, realising as he does so that the stone portal is smaller than it appeared at first!

Portal to the Other Side

There's probably still more to see here, but time is running out and I'm getting hungry (a lot of my breakfast ended up on Alan's plate), so I suggest getting some grilled mochi from the guy in a little shack by the main gate as we leave. They're delicious. Chewy, slightly mugwort flavoured, with just a hint of a charcoal.

Isaniwa Shrine

I decide to walk back to the city centre from Ishiteji rather than take a bus, with the intention of stopping at a shrine and another temple (not one of the 88 pilgrimage trail ones) on the way. Isaniwa shrine isn't far from Dogo Onsen station but it's an 18-minute walk downhill from Ishiteji followed by a lot (and I mean a LOT) of steps up to the temple itself. There's a group of calm, cool, refreshed-looking women wearing high heels walking around the shrine, and I'm beginning to think there might have been an easier way to get here than the one I took. They probably drove up and parked in the parking lot next to the shrine. But where's the fun in that?

I'm wandering around an 'Important Cultural Property', which is Hachiman-Zukuri style for any architecture buffs reading this. For the rest of us, it's a traditional vermillion building (which looks like two separate buildings joined together) with pillars, a gabled roof, and a courtyard surrounded by cloisters. The main building was built here in 1667, but the original shrine was built a while before that (some say 1000 years, but I don't know) close to where the Dogo Onsen is now located.

Step by Step by Step by Step

The Shinto deity Hachiman, a god of war and archery, is worshipped here, but he's also one of the Buddhist divine beings, so it's a bit of a hybrid-religion shrine. There's some great artwork of warriors doing things like fighting tigers, lots of brightly painted heads of strange animals, and even a bonsai tree sitting in a pot in the cloisters. It's a nice shrine, but was it worth hiking up all those steps to get here? I think so, yes.

Next on the agenda is Hogonji, a Buddhist temple up a hill somewhere nearby. It's reported to have a nice rock garden and buildings which were rebuilt after burning down in 2013, but both Alan and I are tired and hungry so we abandon that plan and go for lunch instead.

Imperial Bath Time!

After a trip back to the ryokan for a shower, I'm now at the Dogo Onsen Asaka-no-Yu annex, which is about a five-minute walk from the old onsen next to a shopping arcade. It's a beautiful building, completed in 2017, with gleaming white walls and wooden beams. A balcony decorated with floral paper lanterns overlooks the courtyard, which is covered with a temporary art installation of brightly coloured floral floor tiles. A small red bridge spans a stream, connecting the courtyard to a small shrubbery. In 596 a Prince Shotoku visited Dogo and sang a song about camelias, so I think that's what the bushes are. At the entrance to the annex is a ticket office where people can pay to visit the public baths and use the relaxation rooms for an hour or so.

Alan and I enter the building and are welcomed at the reception desk, asked to place our shoes in the lockers and take a seat in the huge, brightly lit, modern foyer. We're not waiting long before our hostess appears and gestures for us to follow her up to the second floor, where our private onsen experience will take place.

She leads us to a room with tatami mats on the floor, an antique-looking lamp in the corner, and a low table with cushions to sit on. There's a basket containing folded Yukata by the wall. We take a seat, and our hostess kneels by the table. After some bowing (she seems quite nervous) she shows us her phone screen. It says 'I'm sorry I do not speak any English'. That certainly explains some of her anxiety. I tell her we understand a little Japanese, but please speak slowly. She's very happy to hear this, and immediately launches into rapidly spoken explanations and instructions. Fortunately there's eight pages of laminated instruction sheets in English laid out on the table, so I don't get totally overwhelmed trying to follow what she's saying.

The condensed version is: Choose a robe in which to bathe. Go into the Imperial Room beyond the sliding wooden doors. Do not use any soap or shampoo, but rinse using fresh water collected in little buckets. Bathe wearing the robes like the Imperial Family used to do, then wring them out well and place them in the basket in the antechamber. If we want to try the public onsens on the main floor, dress in one of the yukata provided and head downstairs. There is a public relaxation room down the corridor with a balcony, or we can phone her and she will bring tea to our room. We have 90 minutes, starting from… Now!

I don't think I've ever gotten dressed to take a bath before, so today's experience is a unique one. I think the Imperial Family were probably better at it than Alan and me, as we're really struggling to stop our 'privacy garments' from floating upwards. I think there's a few accidentally X-rated selfies I'll have to delete later lol. We're enjoying the imperial experience so much that I don't think we'll have time to check out the public onsens on the first floor, which are decorated with murals made out of porcelain panels inspired by traditional waka poetry. I will, however, take a wander to look into the courtyard from the relaxation room balcony, and fan myself while drinking tea and eating delicate snacks in our private room before it's time to check out.

This was an amazing experience, and I'm very grateful to the tourist office lady who booked it for me.

Bathing Like an Emperor

Bath time is over, and Alan and I are now taking a leisurely stroll around the neighbouring streets, looking in stores and maybe buying a trinket or two, filling the time until we have to return to the ryokan for dinner. I've just bought two small, cute towels, which will come in useful when we arrive at a skywalk footbath overlooking Dogo Onsen Honkan.

But first, a quick detour to look at the pretty Yu Shrine (wood beams, white walls), where two important deities are enshrined. As far as I understand, 'enshrinement' in cases like this means there's a hidden statue somewhere, or there's some religious artifacts related to the deities, or it's simply a place where designated deities are worshipped or prayed to. The heavenly beings Onamuchi no Mikoto and Sukunahikona no Mikoto have been somehow attached to the Dogo Onsen and Yu Shrine since the 10th century. The shrine was originally built in a different location and moved here after the onsen was buried by an earthquake. Now if the waters in the Dogo Hot Spring stop flowing it can all be resolved by doing some singing and dancing rituals here while praying to the two enshrined deities. I believe this was last done in the 1700's by a feudal lord after an earthquake.

Happy Feet

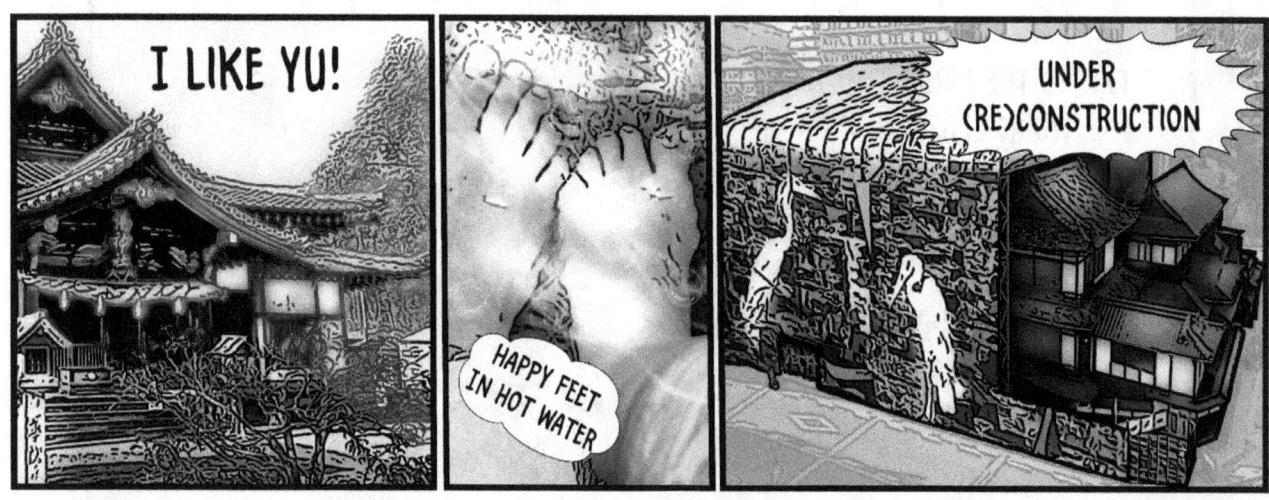

So now I'm sitting on a bench soaking my feet in a trench of hot water which flows directly from the spring, typing notes on my phone, and hoping I don't accidentally drop it into the footbath. There's a little garden behind me, and in front there would be a great view of Dogo Onsen Honkan if it wasn't mostly covered by a colourful tent while undergoing renovations.

Dining on Delicacies

I'm writing my final notes of the day after another multi-course dinner served in our room, followed by a final soak in our private onsen.

Dinner included a couple of treats for us today, prepared specially for us by the chef. It was, of course, another exceptional meal, beautifully presented and perfectly cooked. Or not cooked, if it was supposed to be raw of course. I have to admit I struggled a bit more than usual with tonight's menu. The chopped whelk served inside a shell was something I've not encountered before, and neither Alan nor I could chew it enough to swallow more than one tiny piece each. The raw fugu (which Alan loved) must be an acquired taste, and I really didn't like it. But the crowning moment for me was a local sea bream speciality...

Something Fishy is Going On

I've really enjoyed my two nights in this luxury ryokan, but I'm ready to return to reality. I've been made to feel very welcome here, but I'm happy to return to cheaper accommodations, a filling buffet breakfast, and dinner in an inexpensive restaurant with pictures on the menu.

Marugame

shiro ato ya
furui no shimizu
mazu towa n
At the castle ruins fresh water from the ancient well takes me back to times long past
(Matsuo Basho)

Today we're on the move again, heading to Takamatsu in Kagawa. According to the tracking app on my phone our luggage is already on its way there, having left the hotel very early this morning. I'm taking a bit of a detour though, stopping at the castle town of Marugame on the way there. I've already got a reserved seat ticket, so all I have to do is check out of this hotel, catch a tram to the JR station and jump on a train for the next leg of the Shikoku adventure.

Marugame Castle

After an uneventful three-hour train ride I'm in Marugame! It was a 15 minute walk to the bottom of Turtle Hill (where the castle is) from the train station, pausing for some badly overcooked udon noodles for lunch along the way. I hope the castle is better than the food! I can see it on the hilltop, a bright white building against a clear blue sky. It's one of Japan's 'original' castles, even though it was demolished around 1615 and rebuilt in 1660.

The walk up to the castle is long and steep! Very steep. I was actually considering stopping for a while under the pretence of admiring the view and the pretty trees, but three grannies just marched past me, going at an impressive pace. If they can do it I can do it too! Perhaps I shouldn't mention that one of them is bent over at almost 90 degrees at the waist and supporting herself with a stick? It might make me look a bit pathetic in comparison.

So, I've made it the top of the hill. I'm hot, tired and sweaty, but I'm here. The view is great but I'm not convinced that the castle itself was worth the climb. All the buildings except the keep and a couple of gates have burned down over the years and weren't rebuilt, so there's really not a lot to see. Yes, the tenshu is pretty, but it's nothing I've not already seen before.

I suspect I'm a bit hot and tetchy. I didn't eat much of breakfast, lunch was meh, and the castle is barely a castle at all. It turns out that Alan is also feeling the strain today, so when we arrive back at the bottom of the hill he cools down with an ice cream and I cheer myself up with candy-coated strawberries on a stick. I'm now in a much better mood and can appreciate the pretty yellow flowers on the trees (I assume they're not cherry blossoms) and admire the castle Tenshu from afar.

Steep Hill and Strawberries

Goshoji

Fortified by the candied strawberries, I wander back to the station and hop on a train to Utazu, home of Goshoji, Temple 78 on the pilgrimage trail. I hope it's more exciting and less strenuous than Marugame castle! It's known locally as the 'warding off evil' temple because of a wooden statue which wards off evil, or something like that. Honestly, I find a lot of the temple folklore a bit confusing. I was also a bit confused about how to get here. The 'bus' from the station to the temple turned out to be an unmarked white minivan, but a couple of old ladies assured me it was actually public transport and not a private van from a retirement residence.

There was a bit of a hike up a hill after the minivan dropped me off, leading to a very nice temple gate. The complex courtyard is surrounded by lovely wooden shrines, and I can see three carved monkeys sitting on top of one of them. The sound of drumming emanates from the main temple, adding to the serene beauty of this complex. There's a lovely garden which will probably be even nicer a bit later in the season, with views over the Seto Inland Sea. There are, of course, stone Jizo wearing red bibs in addition to a multitude of other religious figures carved out of stone. The temple bell has a story attached to it. Legend says that this bell rings for longer than any other because a strange man put something into the cast when the bell was being formed. I didn't hear it being bonged, so I can't tell you if this is true or not.

Monkey Business

There's a few small torii gates, some Tanuki statues (shape-shifting racoon-dog deities) and a plump real-life fluffy cat sitting next to steps leading down under a statue of Amida Nyorai, the principal deity of this temple. And this is where things get really interesting! There's thousands (no exaggeration!) of tiny gold statues of the goddess down here in a dimly lit crypt. Some of them have small teddy bears or other toys perched on them, and there's the occasional small bunch of flowers adorning the shelves. It's a bit eerie down here!

Time has flown by, and I have to leave Goshoji and head to Takamatsu. Ahead of me is a 20 minute walk back to the station followed by a limited express JR train ride (it will take about an hour), a local train to Kawara Machi station, and finally a bit more walking to get to Wing International Hotel.

Waiting for the train, Alan offers me a piece of an old granola bar he found lurking at the bottom of his backpack. It looks like it's seen better days, but I accept it gratefully. He suggests we grab dinner at the JR station when we arrive in Takamatsu then I can go to bed as soon as we arrive at the hotel if I want. That sounds like a really good idea. Somehow it feels like it's been a very long day.

Takamatsu, Kagawa

Haruno-umi
Hinemosu-Notari
Notarikana
Spring ocean swaying gently all day long
(Yosa Buson)

I didn't actually go straight to bed upon arriving at the hotel, where my luggage was waiting for me in my room. Instead, I've had a long soak in a hot bath, which revitalised me enough to tell you a bit about Kagawa before going to sleep.

Kagawa, the smallest of the four prefectures in Shikoku, is located in the north east, and faces Okayama on Honshu across the Seto Inland Sea. It's popular in summer thanks to a low amount of rain and white sandy beaches with clear water. Ritsurin gardens (more about that later) is popular year round, but especially in the spring and fall. Kagawa has relatively mild winters, making it a nice spot to escape to for winter illuminations.

So, why am I here? Well, unsurprisingly perhaps, there's some pilgrimage trail temples located in Kagawa, and I'm hoping to visit at least one of them. The best known one here is Okuboji, temple 88, the very last temple on the route. It's at the top of a mountain and involves a long 'contemplative climb' to get there, so I'll give that one a miss. I also won't be going to Kompirasan Shrine (also known as Kotohiragu) in Kotohira, which isn't one of the 88 temples but is famous for the many, many steps up a shop-lined pathway to the main temple, with many more steps leading to another temple even further up the mountain. It sells 'yellow charms of happiness', which might be needed after climbing 1,368 steps lol. I'm a bit sad that it's not on this trip's itinerary, especially since I didn't get there the last time I was in Kotohira. Instead of climbing the steps, I was busy changing my itinerary because a big earthquake struck Kumamoto, which is where I was supposed to be heading next.

Ferries run from various ports in Kagawa to islands in the Seto Inland Sea. The best known one is Naoshima, which has outdoor art installations and is the site of the yearly Setouchi Triennale art festival. Shodoshima is known for its prize-winning olive plantations and a Mediterranean-like climate, while Honjima, Ogijima and Megijima are small but full of history. I'm hoping to do some island-hopping while I'm here, weather permitting. However, the long-range forecast says rain is heading this way...

I'm going to be based in Takamatsu for the next few days, which is the capital city of Kagawa. A whopping 78% of the city was destroyed by bombs during World War II and was rebuilt after the war ended. It forms a semi-circle around Takamatsu Port, which was the main point of entry into Shikoku before the Seto Ohashi Bridge was constructed in 1988.

This isn't my first time in the prefecture, but my previous stay in Takamatsu was fairly brief and I got around by taxi (quite an expensive choice!) or on foot. There are much better ways to move around the city if you're not in a rush. Buses can get you to most places, but honestly it's easier to use the local Kotoden railway, which starts close to the JR train station, runs through the city, and goes as far as Kotohira.

Takamatsu airport, which is where I'll be heading when I leave Shikoku in a few days, is about 40 minutes drive away from the JR station (25 minutes from somewhere close to my hotel) and is easily accessed using the airport limousine coach.

The top attractions here are the famous Ritsurin Gardens and Takamatsu Castle, but I'm hoping to also get to less well known places such as Yashima (the site of a historic battle) and Shikoku Mura (an open air museum). There's an onsen area in the south of Takamatsu, but that's not on my to-do list.

Food!

Kagawa (previously known as Sanuki) is nicknamed the 'udon prefecture' in honour of the regional delicacy Sanuki noodles. These are thick with flat edges instead of being round. I'm not an expert, but these noodles reputedly have superb lustre and elasticity. Kagawa produces (and consumes) more noodles than any other region in Japan. It even has an Udonnoww mascot, a goblin which ate so many noodles that its brain turned into noodles.

On a previous trip to Kagawa I signed up for a noodle making class in the old town of Kotohira. It was a fun afternoon of mixing, kneading and dancing on dough (in a sealed plastic bag), which we formed into noodles and ate for dinner in the noodle school dining room. It was, of course, delicious.

Noodles aren't the only regional speciality in this prefecture, which is also known for olive products, olive-fed Wagyu Beef (fed on bi-products from the olive-oil industry), and honetsukidori (seasoned chicken pieces cooked on the bone). And, of course, citrus fruits.

Kagawa Cuisine

Tanuki Tales Temple, and an Old Village

Tsurigane ni
tomarite hikaru
hotaru kana
Settled on the temple bell – a glowing firefly
(Masaoka Shiki)

I know I've only just arrived in Takamatsu, but I'm heading a bit out of town today, going to Mount Yashima to see a temple and a village museum. It will take about an hour to get there using a local train line followed by a bus. The weather forecast is predicting lots of rain later in the week, so today might be the last sunny one for a while, perfect for an outdoor excursion.

Yashima

Today I'm visiting my final Shikoku Pilgrimage temple, Yashima, number 84. Getting here has been a bit of fun. I took the train to Yashima as planned, and as I exited the train station I could see the bus I needed sitting not far away. Other people spotted it too, and started to run towards it. I assumed they knew something I didn't, so I began to run too. We all boarded then sat in a stationary bus for over five minutes before it finally set off up the long winding road to the temple. The bus driver probably thought we were quite funny.

Busy Going Nowhere

It's a bit cool at this mountaintop temple, and I wish I'd brought a sweater with me. It's an interesting place though. There was a historic battle here around 1185, and the treasure house (there's a fee to enter)

has various relics from that era. The sign outside the treasure house says 'enter here, then pay for your ticket at the main office' or something like that, so after wandering around looking at the old swords, scrolls and other artifacts I retrace my steps to the wooden building at the entrance to the complex. An old man is sitting quietly writing something, and is startled when he sees me. I show him the leaflet I picked up in the treasure house and ask if I can buy two tickets (Alan is with me, of course). He gets very flustered, but eventually we manage to sort it all out. While I'm in the building I give my pilgrimage book to a lady along with the required 300 yen and get the relevant page stamped. I'm so happy that I bought this book. I know I've only been to a few temples, but it was totally worth the expense. One thing I won't be spending money on, however, is a 1,000yen ($10 Canadian) replica bow and arrow set, which Google translate thinks is evil.

Timeless Treasures

I'm spending quite a lot of time admiring Tanuki statues around the temple courtyard. According to legend, when Kobo Daishi was on his way to Yashima-ji he got lost in a thick mist. An old man wearing a straw hat and a raincoat led him to the temple. This strange man was really a shape-shifting Tanuki sent by a deity to help Daishi. For some reason (don't ask me to explain) these shape-shifters often appear as large raccoon-dogs (Tanuki) with special magical powers, and they enjoy playing tricks on people.

Tiny Tanuki

Tanuki are said to have extra special magical testicles (!) which they use as raincoats or drums in some stories. I can assure you that all the statues here have quite large testicles, but I don't see any of them using them in a strange or unexpected way.

Tall Tanuki

 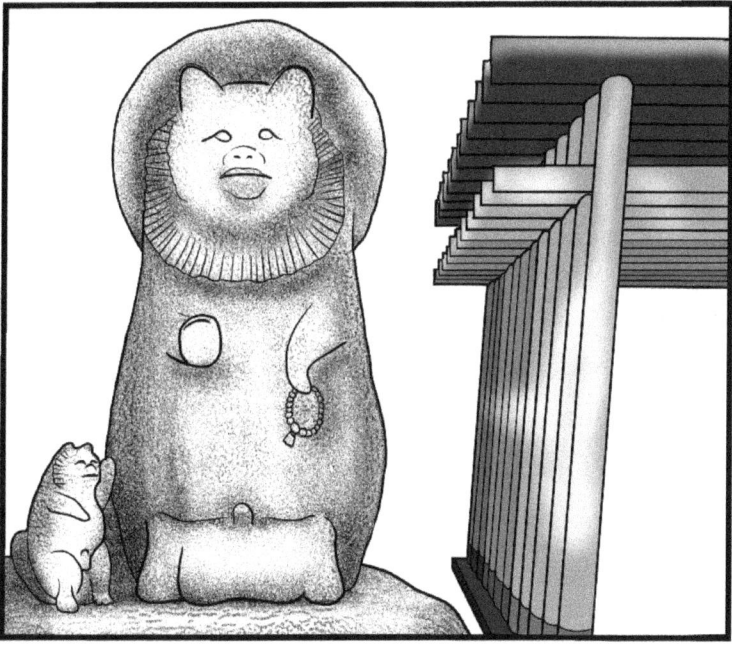

Enough of this – it's time to wander down a country lane in search of the old castle ruins, and to find the pond of blood where soldiers from the historical battle washed their swords.

Tales, and More Tanuki

The pond is peaceful and pretty, with no trace of the violence and bloodshed lost in the mists of time, but I can't seem to find the castle ruins anywhere.

At the end of a lane where I thought the castle ruins might be, all I find are the ruins of a huge government international tourist hotel. I glimpse a young couple cuddling in one of the derelict rooms, surrounded by broken glass and fallen beams.

The views from this mountaintop are lovely. I can understand why a hotel was built here, even though it was obviously unsuccessful as a business. There's a solitary sakura tree here with just a few delicate cherry blossoms remaining on it, looking wilted and battered by the wind. I take a moment to reflect on the brevity of sakura, the impermanence of all things, and fragility of life then head back to the temple grounds in search for a vending machine containing hot tea. There's a limit to how long I can think deep thoughts...

Shikoku Village

I've hopped back on the bus taking me down the mountainside to an outdoor museum containing old buildings from around this island. Many of them were built in the Edo and Meiji periods and carefully moved to Shikoku Village (also known as Shikoku Mura) for preservation. I think there's 30 or so structures here, including houses, workshops and storehouses. One thing I'm looking forward to is an old vine bridge, based on one in the Iya Valley in Tokushima, where I'm not going on this trip. Some reviews say this one is a bit on the scary side.

At the entrance to the museum is a house which looks slightly out of place. It was built for an Englishman and his Japanese wife in 1904 and has been turned into a tearoom.

Wait, what? A tearoom? I know I've recently had tea from a vending machine, but I can't turn down an offer of tea from a teapot served with a slice of carrot cake...

Traditional Tea and Cake

Teatime is over, and it's time to enter the actual museum. It's really pretty in here, and very, very quiet. I'm not sure there's any other tourists here. It's just a shame somewhere this nice doesn't seem to be very popular.

I've wandered up a hill, and the first thing I encounter is the old rope bridge. It's off to the side as an 'optional' route, but of course both Alan and I want to try it. It sways and creaks alarmingly as we cross it one at a time. The structure is reinforced with metal cables, but the large uneven gaps between the randomly shaped tree branch slats added to the sense of danger. It might actually be *real* danger on rainy days when the wooden slats are wet and slippery!

Onwards and upwards! Just a note if you're thinking of coming here, there's a lot of walking. And a lot of it is on uneven wooden steps which are probably slippery when wet. There's warning signs every now and again, only in Japanese, but the cartoon of a slipping foot gets the message across. There's also some signs warning about hornets, snakes and wild boars. I met some boars in the mountains near Kumamoto a few years ago. They weren't very interested in me, which was lucky because those little piggies have very impressive tusks!

As I continue on the walk uphill I see wood-framed round houses with thatched roofs. One has a sign outside saying it contains a traditional sugar cane press, but instead there's a 6ft long glass bottle with a suitcase inside it. Strange but true. Another of the buildings has a huge steamer and a really interesting video. It shows how traditional washi paper was made from steamed tree branches during the winter months as a source of income when it was too cold for farming. There are subtitles on the video in both Japanese and English.

And so the climb continues, past a white wooden lighthouse, ending at the summit surrounded by tulips outside some European-looking houses.

The way back down is as interesting as the journey up, passing a lovely man-made waterfall and peaceful lake, and an outdoor Kabuki theatre brought here from Shodoshima Island. And of course I have to pay a second visit to the bridge because it's way too much fun to only do once.

We're now having a very late lunch in the traditional thatched farmhouse (relocated here from Tokushima) at the entrance to the village. Their speciality is, of course, udon, so it's country-udon for Alan, and more country-udon for me. With, of course, tea.

Bridges, Tulips and Tradition

There's a Haiku for Everything!

tan itto
hechima no mizu mo
ma ni awazu
a quart of phlegm—even gourd water couldn't mop it up
(Masaoka Shiki)

I'm feeling a bit under the weather this evening – snotty nose, sore throat, more tired than I should be after today's activities – so I took a small detour on the way back to the hotel to get cold and flu meds from a drug store. I'm huddled up in bed, dining on a random selection of foody things Alan picked up from a grocery store for me. He's fortifying himself with sake and a supermarket package meal he microwaved in the hotel lobby.

That's all I'm writing for now. I'm going to have a hot bath to hopefully sweat off the virus, followed by an early night dopped up on flu medicine. I'll be back tomorrow.

Feeling Weathered

Ritsurin Gardens

waga kuni wa
kusa sae sakinu
sakura kana
In my province grass blooms too...cherry blossoms
(Kobayashi Issa)

I'm not sure what was in those Japanese cold and flu meds, but I'm feeling positively perky this morning, with no sign of the sniffles. Phew! I'm especially relieved because today is the day Alan and I are returning to one of our favourite spots in Japan – Ritsurin Gardens. This beautiful, tranquil place is the largest 'Cultural Property Garden' in Japan. It dates back to the Edo period, starting as a small garden which now forms one of the corners of the present site, and was expanded by a succession of feudal lords over many years. The total area covers 185 acres – a bit bigger than both the Forbidden City in China (180 acres) or Disneyland (160 acres) if that gives you some idea of the scale – but the actual 'garden' area is about 40 acres (something like 30 American football fields). The rest is the pine-covered slopes of Mount Shuin. It was first opened to the public in 1875 and was designated as a 'Special Place of Scenic Beauty' in 1953.

Ritsurin Koen, literally translated, means chestnut grove park, but it's actually best known for having over 1,000 pine trees, many of which are carefully pruned to look like huge bonsai trees. I remember from a previous visit that one actually started out as a little bonsai tree in a pot. I'll tell you more about it when I find it...

It's a short walk and train ride to the park entrance on a day which is sunny but not too hot. Alan has left his daypack in the lockers by the entrance, bought our tickets and picked up a handy map (in English). He's decided against renting an audio guide. We need to buy tickets for a boat ride on the lake later on, but the office for this is somewhere inside the gardens.

There's reputedly over 300 cherry blossom trees in Ritsurin gardens, but I'm not sure where they all are. The overwhelming colour here is green. Lots and lots of green. It was green when I was here early in the fall, and it's green now in the late spring. I suspect it's always green, even when dusted with mid-winter snow. True, there's a few trees with pale pink blossoms on some trees, but if I'd specifically come here to see sakura I think I would have been disappointed. Perhaps I'm a week too late this year. A good time to come for blossoms might be February or March when the plum grove trees are in bloom.

There's suggested routes on the map, and there's arrows pointing the way in the gardens, but I think I'm just going to wander and enjoy the lakes, bridges and man-made hills. I know there's a folk museum here somewhere, but it's not on my to-do list today. I could easily spend hours slowly walking around here. It's mostly fairly flat, but there's a great view over the lake from the man-made Hiraiho hill, which resembles Mount Fuji. The 'crescent moon' Engetsukyo Bridge looks beautiful from up here, reflected in the waters flowing beneath.

My journey has brought me to the Kikugetsu-tei teahouse on the banks of Nanko Pond. Outside this lovely wooden building, with a veranda looking out over the lake, is the tree I mentioned earlier. It's even got a name! Neagari Goyo-Matsu Pine was given to the resident shogun in 1833 as a little bonsai, and it's been growing in the garden ever since! It's big, beautiful, and propped up in places with wooden poles. I'm going to buy some tea and seasonal snacks, and spend a bit of time sitting on the tatami mats in the teahouse admiring the view.

Contentment

Next on today's relaxed agenda is a boat ride on the lake (I passed the ticket office earlier and booked a time), wearing the obligatory straw hats. Alan and I nestle against each other in the old wooden wasen boat, and a solitary lady sits on the bench in the bow. Our boatman doesn't speak English, but I'm quite happy to be punted around without a commentary. The middle of the pond is the best spot from which to admire the gardens, with the bonus of seeing turtles sitting on rocks and a crane hunting fish in the shallow waters around a small island.

I'm taking a short stroll around the north garden before heading out, which is nice but probably looks better at other times of the year. It was made during the Meiji era and is more 'western' in style. There's thousands of irises here but they aren't in bloom at the moment. It's where the park's largest pond is located, which was used as a site for duck hunting in the Edo period.

It feels like it's only been a short visit, but in reality I've been here for hours. Time well spent.

Beauty at its Best

RITSURIN GARDENS

We had lunch in Ritsurin Gardens part way through today's wanderings – udon for me, and udon in curry sauce for Alan – so tonight we're trying to actually NOT have noodles for dinner. We've taken a bit of a chance and walked into a random izakaya, which serves pub-style food. I've ordered various veggie dishes, and Alan has chosen what he thinks is chicken and pork on skewers, but neither of us can work out exactly which parts of the animals they are. Google is very helpfully (!) suggesting things like triangle, momo, free-range chicken (ok!), hormone and sputum, and we've finally worked out that one is probably asparagus bacon (he doesn't like asparagus). Nothing on the menu carried the 'please don't suffocate' warning like we saw on some mochi back in the park, so it's probably edible, right?

Wrong.

After a lot of chewing, and some very furrowed brows, Alan has declared most of the things-on-a-stick to be 'not food' and is helping me to eat my tofu and veggies while he consoles himself with a large beer.

We'll probably never know what he ordered lol.

Dangerous Dining

Rainy Day Wanderings

Hitowatashi
Okureta hito ni
Shigure kana
Late for the ferry he stands alone in drizzling rain
(Yosa Buson)

It looks like our final day in Takamatsu is going to be a bit of a wet one. The original plan was to take a ferry to some of the islands off the coast of Shikoku, but it really doesn't look like a good day to wander around looking at outdoor art installations. Perhaps I'll get to the islands on a future trip to Japan by taking a ferry there from mainland Honshu. But that doesn't mean today is a total wash-out. There's always things to do, even on a day like this.

Takamatsu Art Museum

Takamatsu art museum is only a few minutes walk from the hotel, most of which is through the covered shopping arcade followed by a short dash with an umbrella. As I enter, a group of ladies in Kimonos wave and beckon me over to a desk on the right. I'm a bit confused because I can see the museum ticket office straight ahead of me, but I head over to where the ladies are. "Welcome! Would you like some tea?" I look at Alan and he nods. We rarely turn down the offer of a cup of tea. "Please, sit down!" I plop onto one of the soft square stools and a lady brings me a tray of green tea with a lovely sakura shaped snack. She explains that this is a special exhibition of calligraphy artwork by a local lady who has studied in many places and is well known in Shikoku. The artist herself is visiting today. Would I like to meet her? Of course I would! The lady bustles off and returns with a tiny woman wearing a lovely kimono, and she's very excited to meet Alan and me. She's met a Canadian before, and apparently they were very nice. We talk a little about her work, and learn that she first started doing this style of calligraphy after visiting a similar exhibition when she was younger and couldn't read any of it. She's delighted when I say I can't read her writing but find it beautiful. It takes many years of studying and diligent practice to master this art style, and she's happy I like it.

After a lot of bowing, Alan and I extract ourselves from the calligraphy display and head into the main museum, taking care not to step on the plastic artwork strips covering a large part of the floor. We kept our tickets from Ritsurin Gardens and as a result get a discount on today's gallery tickets.

There's a lot less art here than I expected. The main floor didn't take long to tour, and I nearly missed one of the art installations because I thought it was the door to a storage closet, and another because I thought it was just a chair. Upstairs is a 'citizen's gallery' and some of the pieces are really good. Others, not so much so. The website says this gallery includes over 1,700 works of art and I wonder if I'm missing something, but I'm ready to head off on other rainy day adventures.

Arty Antics

Sunport

After a bit of wandering, I arrive at Sunport, a business and shopping district not far from the JR train station. The last time I was here it was bright and sunny, but today the world looks very different from the top of the Symbol Tower. This is the tallest building in Takamatsu, and it took a bit of hunting to find the correct elevator to get to the rooftop. It's very, very windy up here, and the entire building seems to be swaying. Looking out over the choppy waters I think it was a wise choice not to go on a ferry trip to the islands today, and it's quite a relief to get back inside away from the gales. I'm heading down to the shops on the lower level to look for a Slowpoke to squish into my already over-stuffed suitcase. I don't know why, but Slowpoke is a 'tourism character' in Kagawa prefecture and appears on things like airport coaches and trains.

Sunless Sunport

Takamatsu Castle

Not far from Sunport are the ruins of Takamatsu castle, which I visited a few years ago so I and don't feel the urge to revisit today. It's one of Japan's waterfront castles with a saltwater moat, like the one in Imabari. There's some ruins, a tenshu and a pretty garden, which probably looks less pretty on a grey rainy day like today.

Reminiscing About Ruins

I think the rest of the day is going to be spent wandering around the shopping arcades followed by a Coco Curry dinner, beer and a hot bath. It's not how I imagined spending my final day in Shikoku, but I'm sure there will be fun things to see. For example, there's a sign for a karada (body) factory over there, and I (still!) have no idea what that is, so my imagination is going wild. Alan is wandering over to a large plastic cat to pose for a photo. It's going to be an entertaining afternoon.

Fun with no Sun

Sayonara Shikoku

mono kaite
ōgi hikisaku
nagori kana
I wanted to write my farewell poem on a fan – it's suddenly broken
(Matsuo Basho)

There wasn't a lot of excitement to write about today, but I'm doing a quick catch-up before heading off to bed. The day started with a short walk from the hotel to the bus stop to catch the airport limousine (coach) to Takamatsu airport, which was about a 25 minute ride. Checking in at the airport went without drama – no problems with the carry-on luggage, no flashing lights on the body scanners – and our flight to Haneda went as scheduled. It was a bit bumpy at times but the view through the window was great for most of the 1 ½ hour flight.

We arrived in Haneda, caught the second airport limousine of the day, and made the hour or so trip to Narita airport. A really tough-looking kinda scary guy was sitting in the seat across the aisle from me, but he seemed a lot less intimidating when he started watching cute bunny videos on his phone. I looked over to see what Alan was doing. He was watching cat videos.

Dinner was delicious, eaten in a casual Japanese restaurant at the airport while gazing through the window. Then today's journey was completed by taking a train from the airport to Narita Station, just a few minutes walk from the hotel.

This long, convoluted journey was not part of the original travel plan, but I get a bonus day tomorrow to do a bit of exploring around Narita so I'm not too unhappy about it. I suspect Air Canada will give me a discount off my next trip because of all the changes they made to this one. (Yes, they did!)

And now, to bed in the APA Hotel Keisei Narita Ekimae. It's a bit run down but it's inexpensive, serves breakfast (for a fee), and it's close to the train station. It also has a shuttle bus to and from the airport, but not at a convenient time for me.

Flying Away, But Not Too Far

173

Narita

Uchiyama ya
tozama shira zu no
hana zakari
Inside the temple visitors cannot know cherries are blooming
(Matsuo Basho)

Today is a bonus day in Japan, so I'm going to make the most of it. My first flight doesn't depart until mid-afternoon, giving me a bit of time to play with after checking out of the hotel and putting my luggage in their storage room. So, one last temple, and maybe a tiny bit of shopping...

Naritasan Shinshoji

It's taken about 20 minutes to walk from the hotel to Naritasan Shinshoji, a large Buddhist temple complex which was first built somewhere around 940, although many of the buildings are much more recent. People recommend spending three hours or so here, but I'll have to do a shorter visit even though there's lots of things to see including five 'Important Cultural Properties' and a large garden. One of the unusual features of this temple complex is the Okuno-in cave, an 11 metre deep cave in which Dainichi Nyorai (the Cosmic Buddha, or Great Sun Buddha) is enshrined. I assume this means there's a statue of the deity somewhere inside, assumedly with an enraged-looking face and blue skin, if it's the same deity I encountered in Thailand. Anyway, the doors to the cave are only open from July 7th to 9th every year so I won't be able to go inside and check.

I enter the complex through an impressive gate (built in 2008) and carry on, past a fishpond with turtles in it, to the Niomon and guardian statues. It's really busy in here compared to anywhere I went to in Shikoku. There's even groups of people being taken around by a guide. There's a very popular stall selling charms nearby. It's offering a large selection, covering everything from longevity, academic (and various other kinds of) luck, victory, safety in traffic, disease healing and many more.

You can buy books to collect stamps from six of the buildings in the temple complex, similar to the book I bought for the 88 temples on Shikoku. The books are 20,000 yen and each stamp is 300 yen, so I think I got good value for my money when I bought my much bigger Shikoku pilgrimage one.

Seeing Shinshoji

There's so much to see here, and a lot of it is brightly painted and intricately decorated. I can hear a ceremony going on in the main temple, which is where I think a big statue carved by Kobo Daishi is located, but it will have to wait for another visit. A few steps away across a courtyard there's a beautifully ornate pagoda decorated in red, green, blue and gold. Dragon heads stick out of the gables and human figures are carved above the doorway. A sign says there's five Buddhas enshrined inside, but there's railing all the way round so I can't go in.

Nearby is an old bronze statue of a lizard-like dragon climbing a pole, and other statues sit in the courtyard shrines. The Issaikyo-do building in the corner contains a brightly coloured highly decorated rotating six-sided bookcase containing thousands of Buddhist scriptures. There's a long, high rock garden behind the main hall (there's toilets near here, FYI) dotted with statues. Not far from there, tucked behind a shrine (I've stumbled upon it by accident), is the Okuno-in cave, but I have to say it doesn't really look like a cave from the outside. Perhaps I'll have to schedule a visit back here one year in July so I can look inside.

It seems like whatever you need to pray about, there's a shrine or temple here that will meet your needs. Marriage? Go to the Komyodo Hall. Recovery from illness or want a healthy long life? Head over to Loudon, the newest temple here. If you have an exorcism request, Shadako Hall is where you need to be!

At the highest point of the temple complex sits the Great Pagoda of Peace, built in 1984. It's white with red wooden beams, and an ornate green roof. There's an entrance to the park opposite the pagoda, and I regret not having enough time to visit it today. Next time. Maybe.

I've been walking for what seems like ages around the temple complex, pausing to read the many information signs which are written in English, but I've not lingered too long at any of the buildings. My careful planning has left me enough time to climb the steps to the Shusse Inari (fox) shrine. This is where worshipers pray for success, especially in their careers. It's a brightly coloured place, with paper lanterns and flags blowing in the breeze, and even though it's not as busy as Shinshoji there's quite a few people here. I can see some stone fox statues in metal cages, but I don't know why. It's not like they're going to bite people or try to escape. Anyway, it's a colourful lively shrine and worth popping into for a few minutes.

There's stalls selling small fox statues and edible gifts which can be placed on the shine as offerings to the gods. I'm buying a fox for myself, just in case it really does make careers more successful. If you've bought this book perhaps I have the Inari to thank for it... but if you leave me a nice review wherever you bought it from I'll be grateful to you, not the fox.

Feeling Foxy

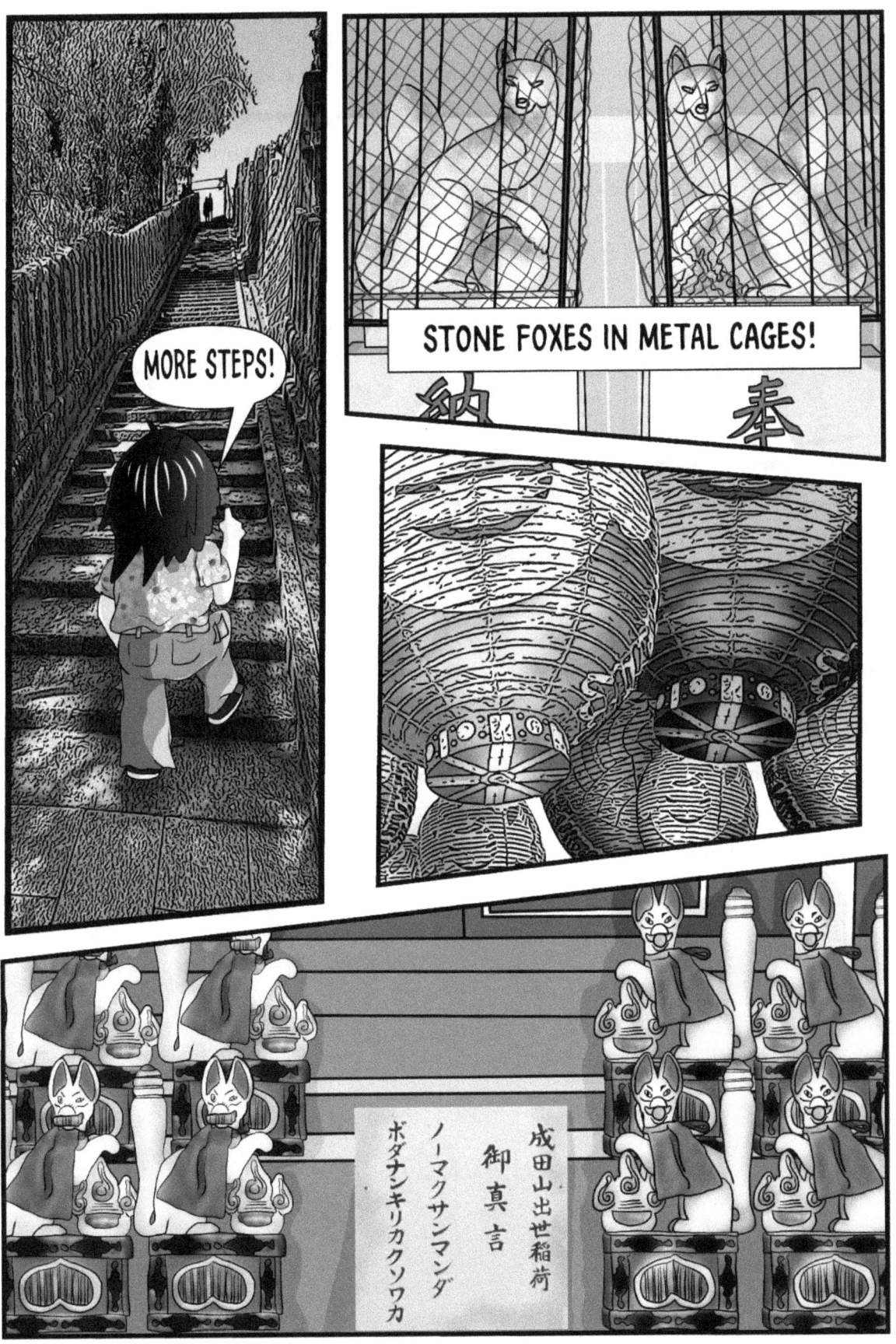

Narita Omotesando

I briefly check out the market stalls in a courtyard next to the main temple complex then head off down Omotesando street, conducting a last-minute search for something I want to buy. On every trip to Japan so far I've bought a solar-powered bowing or wobbling figure such as a lady in a kimono or a sumo wrestler, but I didn't see any while in Shikoku. Just as I'm about to give up hope, in a little shop not far from the hotel, I find what I'm looking for. I can't wait to add them to my collection on the fireplace mantle back home.

Bobbles!

And now, sadly, it's time to head back to the hotel, grab my bags, and catch a train to the airport. Narita airport is an interesting place, so there will be fun shops to look at while waiting for the flight to Toronto, and maybe some tasty snacks to nibble on. I'm not really looking forward to the fifteen hour flight, a three hour layover, then another one hour flight followed by a taxi ride, but...

Heading Home

Sometime Later, Back in Canada

Toshi kure-nu
Kasa kite waraji
Haki-nagara
Another year is gone, still wearing my travel hat and straw sandals
(Matsuo Basho)

It's been a few months since I arrived home safe and sound after a fun time in Shikoku. I saw cherry blossoms in bloom. I tasted sweet citrus fruit. I rode on ancient and modern trams, travelled by trains and coaches, walked up many steep steps, visited temples, shrines and castles, saw amazing views, bathed like an emperor, soaked in an onsen, and ate cookies in an English tearoom. Shikoku was great. A bit wet and windy at times, but great nonetheless.

I'm not sure the timing of this adventure was optimal. I travelled March 21st to April 9th, which I think was possibly a week too early to catch Shikoku sakura at its best. Peak cherry blossom blooming varies from year to year, so if you're planning a trip to Japan in the spring check the sakura forecast before booking your flights. If seeing flowers in bloom is the priority, maybe think about Osaka or Kyoto. But if you want shrines, temples, castles and rugged scenery, Shikoku is the place!

I have a few minor regrets about this trip. I didn't have time to visit Tokushima to see the whirlpool rapids in Naruto, or visit Ryozen-ji or Okubo-ji, the first and last temples on the Shikoku pilgrimage trail. I didn't visit the fertility museum in Uwajimaya to see 'interesting' relics, nor did I see the Kappa or Anpanman museums in Kochi prefecture. Rough seas prevented me from going to Naoshima to see the outdoor artworks. If I'd had a car I might have ventured into the countryside to see caves, lakes and rivers, but it was raining a lot when I was there so perhaps it wouldn't have been time well spent after all. I'm not sure Marugame Castle was worth the hike up the hill, but would I have regretted not seeing it? Probably.

As for accommodations, I wish I'd found a conveniently located apartment to rent in Kochi instead of staying at the Dormy Inn, allowing me to cook my own meals for at least part of the trip. The other hotels, including the expensive one (but still cheaper than lower quality Toronto hotels I've stayed in) in Dogo-Matsuyama, were good choices and I would happily stay there again. But overall I think the trip worked out well.

Now, for me, the hard part of the adventure begins – turning my travel notes into a manga/blog book and getting it onto my editor's desk before flying away again. (Spoiler – I missed that self-imposed deadline by six months lol.) I'm taking Alan to Italy so we can celebrate his birthday drinking tea in a restaurant by the Rialto Bridge in Venice. It will be a bit chilly when we're there, so wine on the patio won't be an option. A few months later we're flying to the UK to join Alan's mom, my brother, and my sister-in-law on a cruise around the Azures, following the path of a solar eclipse and celebrating a couple of family birthdays. It's going to be a bit more sedate than some of my adventures, but it sounds like fun.

But first, this book has to be written! Knowing how to start is always tricky, so maybe I'll write a prologue. Hmm. A prologue to a travelogue! Somehow it just feels right. And that probably tells you more about me than you would think...

Final Words

I hope you've enjoyed reading about my Shikoku adventures as much as I've enjoyed writing / drawing the book. Yes, I needed physiotherapy on my drawing hand for a while, but no pain no gain, or something like that? Which reminds me – at the beginning of this book I mentioned that I had a damaged foot. The good news is that it survived Shikoku, and by the time I got back from Italy some months later I no longer needed athletic tape or physiotherapy for it. Hurray!

If you're planning a trip to Japan, I hope I've helped you decide if Shikoku is somewhere you would like to visit. It doesn't have the bright lights of big cities on the mainland, but it has a charm all of its own. If you've already been to the places I visited I hope it brought back happy memories for you.

I'm now trying to decide where to go next. The world is big, and life is short. I want to see as much as I can while I'm young enough and brave enough. Ziplining in Whistler? Done. Riding a camel in the Rajasthan desert? Check. Whitewater rafting with a broken thumb? Pickpocketed in Rome? Yes! (Even PacSafe bags aren't safe, it turns out). Thai cooking class in Bangkok? Eating Stinky Tofu in Shanghai? Visiting an active volcano on Sakurajima? Whale watching in Cape Cod? Twisted an ankle in Vietnam? Been there, done that, and so much more. But there's endless adventures out there waiting to be had. Maybe I'll even find the time to write about some of them.

Karen

The Never Ending Story...

More Books!